Ethical management for the public services

MANAGING THE PUBLIC SERVICES

Series editor: Dr Alan Lawton, Open University
Business School

Ethical management for the public services

Alan Lawton

Open University Press
Buckingham · Philadelphia

Open University Press
Celtic Court
22 Ballmoor
Buckingham
MK18 1XW

email: enquiries@openup.co.uk
world wide web: http://www.openup.co.uk

and

325 Chestnut Street
Philadelphia, PA 19106, USA

First Published 1998

A catalogue record of this book is available from the British Library

ISBN 0 335 19919 4 (pb)   0 335 19920 8 (hb)

Library of Congress Cataloging-in-Publication Data
Lawton, Alan.
    Ethical management for the public services / Alan Lawton.
        p.   cm. — (Managing the public services)
    Includes bibliographical references and index.
    ISBN 0–335–19920–8 (hbk). — ISBN 0–335–19919–4 (pbk)
    1. Public utilities—Management.   2. Industrial management—Moral
and ethical aspects.   I. Title.   II. Series.
HD2763.L35 1998
363'.068—dc21   98–9696
                                                                             CIP

Typeset by Graphicraft Limited, Hong Kong
Printed in Great Britain by Biddles Limited, Guildford and Kings Lynn

This book is for Julie, for her love, her patience and, above all, her courage

Contents

Series editor's preface

Managing the public services is, increasingly, a complex activity where a range of different types of organization are involved in the delivery of public services. Public services managers have had to develop new skills and adopt new perspectives as the boundaries between public, private and voluntary sector organizations become blurred. The management task becomes one of managing ambiguity in an ever-changing world. At the same time, however, there is a certain timeliness to any debate concerning the management of public policies and managers will need to acknowledge the continuing relevance of traditions and the enduring nature of the themes of accountability, responsibility, acting in the public interest, integrity, probity and responding to citizens, clients and customers.

This series addresses key issues in managing public services and contributes to the debates concerning the appropriate role for managers in the public services located within a contested governance arena. Through the use of original research, case studies and commentaries on theoretical models, the books in the series will be of relevance to practitioners and to academics and their students. An underlying theme of the series is the inescapable intertwining of theory and practice such that theory will be tested out in practice and practice will be grounded in theory. Theoretical concepts and models need to be made relevant for the practitioner but at the same time good practice will need to be analysed, tested against theoretical models and disseminated. In this way the series will fulfil its commitments to both an academic and a practitioner audience.

Alan Lawton

Preface

In some senses, it is assumed that managing public services must, by definition, be ethical. After all, the concepts of integrity, probity, accountability and impartiality would feature in most descriptions of the qualities of civil servants, local government officers and those many professionals working in health, education or welfare. Where unethical conduct does occur it is often headline news around the world as bribery and corruption issues, for example, are condemned universally. That they are wrong goes without saying and yet why they are wrong is seldom questioned. Moral philosophy has not featured strongly in the training of public services managers, nor in the teaching of public sector management. Part of the reason for this is the perceived lack of relevance – and the abstract nature – of much moral philosophy. This book seeks to change that perception by presenting theory in an accessible way through case studies, vignettes and questionnaires. In so doing it will encourage practitioners to locate some of the issues that they face on a day-to-day basis within a wider ethical framework. At the same time it will help academics and their students to make relevant their theories and models. Thus, this book is aimed at those who seek to understand and those who seek to practise. For the theoretician, theory only comes alive in concrete situations, in thinking through the implications of a theoretical position, in testing out propositions concerning, for example, human nature. How do we know that these propositions are correct unless we investigate? At the same time, practitioners need to know what principles they are acting on and what guidance will enable them to make a practical choice or decision and avoid 'reinventing the wheel'. The book uses original research in both the UK and Australia and draws upon relevant research from countries elsewhere.

Acknowledgements

This book has had a long gestation period as the author moved over time from being a postgraduate student and tutor of political philosophy to lecturing in public services management. Political philosophy was never forgotten. Throughout this period (over ten years) encouragement to revisit political philosophy and to seek its relevance for public services management has come from a number of former colleagues and friends. Professor Bob Haigh has always appreciated this approach to public services management and his support goes back a long way. More recently, colleagues at the Open University have encouraged an interest in ethics and management. These include Chris Bollom, Sylvia Brown, Lucille Eveleigh, Heather Hamblin, Euan Henderson, Jan Kaufman, Richard Mole and Stephen Pattison. I also acknowledge the encouragement and advice of Professor Len Wrigley.

Finally, I wish to thank Professor Richard Chapman for his valuable comments on an earlier draft of the book. Any errors, lack of consistency or glaring omissions are the responsibility of the author alone.

one

Introduction: the ethics agenda

Key issues

- The changing context within which public services managers operate.
- The scope and scale of these changes for public services managers.
- The ethical implications of these changes.
- The relationship between the theoretical and practical context of public services ethics.

Introduction

'OECD countries are concerned about declining confidence in government. This so-called "confidence deficit" has been fuelled by well-publicised "scandals", ranging from inappropriate actions on the part of public officials, to full-scale corruption' (OECD 1996: 7). So begins the executive summary to the OECD (Organization for Economic Cooperation and Development) report *Ethics in the Public Service*. The public official, working in the public services and concerned with the formulation and delivery of a wide range of public services, has, in recent years, been subject to much criticism. This criticism has come from a number of different sources. Politicians have been critical of public officials because they believe that an intransigent bureaucracy has acted as a brake on economic growth; users have been critical as their expectations have been raised by the publication of standards and rights, which have often not been met, partly as a result of lack of resources; commentators have been critical, comparing the performance of public officials unfavourably with managers working in the private sector.

The conditions and context within which public officials carry out their duties has changed tremendously following:

- The adoption of markets and quasi-markets (this may be termed the market imperative).
- Devolved management responsibility (the fragmentation imperative).
- The creation of business units and cost centres (the fragmentation imperative).
- The adoption of short-term contracts (the anti-career imperative).
- Contracting out and privatization (the public/private interface imperative).
- The exhortations for managers to be more entrepreneurial, flexible and responsive (the managerialism imperative).
- The pressures on limited resources (the cost imperative).
- An increase in demands from what has become known as the customer (the customer imperative).
- The growth in the 'evaluative state' (the audit/performance imperative).

A concern with the size of government borrowing, with the perceived inefficiencies in the public sector, and a belief in the efficiency and effectiveness of the market as an allocator of resources, led many countries to question the role of government. Common issues were raised, such as:

- Is there a core of activity that is best carried out by government?
- Could, and should, services be provided by the private or voluntary sectors?
- Are the present structures and processes of government appropriate to deliver services?
- How can services be responsive to the customer (replacing the notion of the client or the citizen)?
- How can services be delivered more efficiently and effectively?
- Do public officials help or hinder the effective delivery of public services?

Many countries have gone through change programmes (see OECD 1995). The concerns of this book are not with the different ways in which these and similar issues have been addressed, but with the ethical implications for officials that have arisen as a result of these changes. There has been a growing concern, illustrated in the opening quote to this chapter, that the public service ethos, however defined, has been affected in some way by these changes. In the UK the first report of the Nolan Committee (1995) resulted from the concerns of the, then, prime minister, John Major, that 'sleaze' in government would not be tolerated. In a statement to the House of Commons on Tuesday 25 October 1994 in response to 'public disquiet about standards in public life', the prime minister argued for a committee:

'To examine current concerns about standards of conduct of all holders of public office, including arrangements relating to financial and commercial activities, and make recommendations as to any changes in present arrangements which might be required to ensure the highest standards of propriety in public life' (*Hansard* 1994). The wide-ranging terms of reference were to examine the activities of ministers, civil servants, government advisers, MPs and Euro MPs, members of non-departmental bodies and the National Health Service (NHS), elected members and senior managers in local government, and members of quangos. According to the prime minister: 'This country has an international reputation for the integrity and honour of its public institutions. The reputation must be maintained and be seen to be maintained'.

Why did the prime minister feel the need to defend the integrity of UK public institutions? A number of general explanations have been offered to account for the apparent increase in unethical behaviour among public figures. These included the social climate in the 1980s that encouraged greed and self-interestedness and the existence of a new breed of MPs who stretched conventional understandings of proper conduct. However, it is not the focus of this book to examine the supposed decline in the standards of behaviour of individual politicians (see Leigh and Vulliamy 1997). Rather, the book is concerned with the activities of public officials and the extent to which the standards of conduct expected of them may have slipped or changed as a result of changes in the management of public services. William Plowden, a former senior UK civil servant, has argued, for example, that the relationship between ministers and their officials is under threat because of changes in accountability, roles and expectations. Similar fears were expressed by Robert Sheldon MP in evidence given to the Treasury and Civil Service Sub-Committee (1994). Such concerns are not unique to the UK. In response to changes in the management of public services in Australia, Denis Ives, the public service commissioner expressed the belief that: 'There is a need to re-establish the ethos otherwise it is like setting people to drive in the desert without a map' (personal interview, September 1994). The decline or otherwise of the public service ethos is one of the concerns of this book and is examined in Chapter 4.

Such a concern with public services ethics is not new. Confucius extols the merits of the virtuous administrator. Corruption and patronage have long been key issues in such a concern. Anechiarico and Jacobs (1994), for example, examine the history of corruption control in the USA from 1870 to the present day. However, we have also seen a change of language; public officials are now described as managers expected to control budgets, manage staff, seek to be innovative and entrepreneurial, be more responsive to the consumer and so on. This change in language has implications for how those working within the public services perceive themselves and are perceived by others. And yet, the concept of management and that of the manager are not value-neutral terms. Mintzberg (1996) suggests that there are three assumptions that underlie the 'management' view of management:

1 Particular activities can be isolated, both from one another and from direct authority.
2 Performance can be fully and properly evaluated by the use of objective measures.
3 Activities can be entrusted to autonomous professional managers held responsible for performance.

The success of organizations, both in the private sector and the public sector, is predicated upon managers' abilities to respond to a changing environment, to act entrepreneurially, to be innovative and responsive to the customer and so on. Management textbooks are full of prescriptions which advocate the qualities that managers (usually senior) should possess. We examine the nature of managerial competencies and their relationship with the ethical concept of virtue in Chapter 3.

Managerialism itself has been described as an ideology: 'Managerialism is a set of beliefs and practices at the core of which burns the seldom tested assumption that better management will prove an effective solvent for a wide range of economic and social ills' (Pollitt 1993: 1). Pollitt traces the emerging dominance of managerial ideas in the UK and the USA public services and examines how power has been relocated in the hands of those who claim managerial expertise. Similarly, du Gay *et al.* (1996) argue that the discourse of management has come to dominate the language of the public services manager. They argue that the discourse of 'excellence' stresses the importance of individuals acquiring and exhibiting more market-oriented, proactive, and entrepreneurial capacities. Management in the public services has not always been seen in this way. Hodgkinson (1978) distinguishes between administration and management; the former is concerned with policy-making requiring an appreciation of values and high-level skills; the latter is concerned with means, with carrying out tasks which require a low level of skills.

In some ways critiques of managerialism as an ideology have replaced critiques of bureaucracy as an ideology. Both are deemed to be, in some sense, 'bad things'. Such criticisms of bureaucracy were always too general, aimed at the type of civil servant so amusingly depicted in the *Yes Minister* television series. There always was far more to working in the public services than those involved in policy advice at the tip of the pyramid. In the same way, an alternative view of managerialism would argue that managers, particularly those at the front line of service delivery and middle managers, are managing to deliver effective services despite being squeezed by competing demands from a range of stakeholders including government, senior managers, citizens and clients amid a background of resource pressure. In the same way that critiques of bureaucracy often focused upon senior civil servants, critiques of managerialism may be guilty of the same narrow focus.

However, the use of generic terms such as 'the public official' is often not helpful and neither is the term 'the civil servant'. Such terms describe a status rather than inform us what such people actually do. This book will refer to a range of individuals who work within the public services and who are engaged in a range of different activities which include providing policy advice, collecting revenue, managing the delivery of public services through other organizations via contracts, dealing with clients and so on. Such activities are carried out in a wide range of functional areas such as health, education, welfare, security etc. which are provided through a range of bodies acting on behalf of the state at central government and regional government levels. The intention of this book is to capture the diversity, complexity and richness of public services.

The manager in the public services is a complex person of many roles with mixed motives and mixed purposes. However, the generic term 'the manager' will be used in the book: it is recognized that many of the traditional professionals in the public services now manage people, budgets and information. Where it is appropriate, the book will examine the activities of professionals *qua* professionals rather than in their management roles. A key issue here is the extent to which, as a result of their management role, something of the professional ethos has been lost. We investigate this in Chapters 4 and 5. Managing in the public services is a complex task, involving a range of different stakeholders both inside and outside the organization. These activities and relationships take place against a background of:

- existing organizational practices;
- the expectations of different stakeholders;
- existing social, political and economic practices;
- current and past notions concerning the appropriate role for government.

The book locates the ethical dimension to the activities of public services managers within the wider context of organizational and societal practices. In recognizing the complexity of the task, the sympathies of the book lie with those working within the public services. The book seeks to examine the practices, the pressures, the temptations and the context within which ethical issues arise and to provide guidelines for making sense of some of these issues while recognizing that decisions are often required when little information is available or there are insufficient resources of time or money. Ethical issues arise not just in the context of dilemmas – Chapter 2 examines the notion of what constitutes an ethical issue for the public services manager. However, as a starting point, a number of assumptions are made concerning the activities that public services managers engage in and the relationships that managers have with a range of stakeholders both internal and external to the managers' organization.

Assumption 1

That managers in the public services perform a number of different functions including the collection of revenue, the delivery of services, regulation of service delivery by other agencies and policy advice. These functions are performed within a range of organizational settings including local authorities, government departments and agencies and, increasingly in the UK context, the voluntary and private sectors, and these functions and settings will change over time. Not only that but the question of what functions are performed will usually be an act of political choice.

Assumption 2

That managers in the public services engage in a number of different relationships with a range of stakeholders and that these relationships will vary in form, content and scope. For example, a manager's relationship with a client may be different from that with a customer. Typically, such relationships will be concerned with obligations, duties, rights, agreements (formal and informal), loyalty, accountability and responsibility. Thus, the official whose primary relationship is with politicians and who offers policy advice will be, in principle, characterized by 'speaking truth to power' (see, for example, Heclo and Wildavsky 1981). The skills required will be in marshalling evidence, providing options, evaluating options, and presenting findings. In contrast a front-line manager in a benefits agency may have an impersonal relationship with 'cases' and be circumscribed by formal rules. At the same time such relationships will take place against a background of resource constraints.

Assumption 3

The context within which such relationships take place varies and determines how such relationships are conducted. This context will include:

- hierarchies, markets and networks;
- wider social practices which determine acceptable and unacceptable behaviour on the part of public services managers;
- professional standards and codes of conduct;
- conventions concerning the role and status of managers within society.

If these assumptions are reasonable then delivering public services is a complex business in terms of what is provided, who is to provide it and how it is to be provided. It follows that we should not expect the management of public services to be uniform even within the same organization. For example, those managers charged with carrying out statutory responsibilities may have different views and values concerning public services compared with those managers who are involved in non-statutory services such as economic development or the provision of leisure and recreation facilities. Such issues arise because of the roles played by public services managers, and include:

- In the relationship with politicians where are accountability and responsibility located?
- What motivates those working in the public services to place the interests of the polity as a whole before their own interests?
- What will ensure that the power entrusted to public services managers is not abused?
- How can responsibility be ascribed to public services managers when it is often difficult to isolate the performance of individual managers?

The last point is examined further by Thompson (1980) and is discussed in Chapter 7.

The questions raised in the above list are not unique to the UK or even those administrative systems based on the Westminster model.

The comparative dimension

According to the OECD (1996: 14): 'Despite the differences amongst countries – both cultural and in terms of political and administrative systems – there appears to be growing convergence in what is seen as "good and proper" behaviour'. In a study covering Australia, the Netherlands, New Zealand, the UK, the USA, Finland, Mexico and Norway, the OECD found a number of similarities and some common directions for ethics management in the public services, particularly in terms of procedures for whistleblowing and codes of conduct. At the same time, managers are increasingly aware of 'best practice' elsewhere and recognize that different solutions may be offered to similar problems. There appears to be a growing recognition that much can be learned from management practices elsewhere. Likewise, the plurality of practices – not just across countries but between different levels of government, programmes and functions – is recognized (see Peters 1991; Hood 1996). Focusing on a comparative dimension will help to separate the peripheral and the temporary from the enduring and will help in developing a satisfactory local solution to universal and perennial problems.

An ethical framework reflects, and is reflected in, political, social and economic environments. What is deemed acceptable behaviour in political, economic or social life will be based upon some notion of fairness, equity, justice, duty or obligation. Of course these notions are not static and will change both over time and between different countries with different political, religious, economic and social contexts. This is where the thorny problems of ethical relativism are raised. As public sector organizations operate across national boundaries or interact with supra-national organizations such as the OECD or the European Union, what are the considerations that inform our relationships with other cultures? Do we accept that, for example, in order to do business with country X we have to pay bribes, even though we might find it unacceptable in our own culture?

There is a constant interplay between the personal, the economic and the social and, as Fukuyama (1995) has argued, this will depend upon concepts such as trust, which acts as a bedrock for political, social and economic life. There will be variations depending upon cultural and religious beliefs. In Asia, for example, loyalty to superiors and honouring authority are valued. In East India, managerial leadership at lower levels tends to be paternalistic and autocratic and power-sharing with subordinates and workers is viewed as a weakness. In Latin America the practice of handing out gratuities or bribes for getting something done is legal and an expected form of doing business. Nepotism is not considered to be unethical (see Hopkins 1997).

Throughout this book international comparisons will be drawn, where appropriate, and relevant material from a range of countries will be used. We can learn from others and hope that understanding can be shared among those living in a shrinking world. The enduring nature of ethical issues around the world, particularly the high profile ones such as police corruption, patronage and bribery, makes the comparative approach appropriate. At the same time we should be aware that issues concerning fundamental values are likely to be relevant. Some systems of public administration, for example, take on a particular character, such as the legalistic character of public service in Germany, and certain kinds of behaviour will be deemed to be acceptable as a result.

Theory and practice

How can ethical theory help managers in their practical activity? Can theory provide the manager with a set of guidelines to be taken into consideration when faced with a decision? Theories can operate at different levels of abstraction, such as 'trial-and-error' which represents 'theory in use'. As Watson (1996: 325) argues: 'When managers' actions do reflect their theoretical ideas, there need not necessarily be an explicit or conscious deriving of action decisions from abstract principles'. This book takes the view that theory can help find a reasoned and systematic approach to ethical problems and can inform the practical judgement needed to make decisions. Such judgement requires knowledge. Oakeshott (1962) makes a distinction between two kinds of knowledge: technical and practical. Technical knowledge can be learned through, for example, a correspondence course but practical knowledge reflects a tradition of practice or experience through which knowledge is acquired.

Oakeshott uses the illustration of the good cook, who is not just somebody who can follow a recipe but somebody who is experienced in the practice of cooking itself and who has acquired expertise through experience. This view is reflected in Sisson's (1959) book on the spirit of British government administration which argues that the civil servant '... is a man[sic] who has been trained to a practical operation, not to the exposition of a theory or a search for truth' (p. 23). Of course, this view of administration is one that has been associated with the higher Civil Service and it may be criticized on the grounds that it is an inherently conservative view and does not allow for new ideas or radical change. There is the danger of group-thinking emerging, of a paradigm forming where a set of beliefs and assumptions held in common throughout the organization is taken for granted. However, a recurring theme throughout this book is the existence of social and organizational practices which inform the activities of public services managers.

Theorists may offer elaborate and well-designed models but the practitioner may ask, 'What use is this to me?' The practitioner might argue that what is important is not necessarily the truth or degree of probability of a theory but its utility. The practitioner will be interested in the tests of acceptability, suitability, and feasibility: acceptability in terms of satisfying the demands of key stakeholders; suitability in terms of appropriateness for this or that particular organization; feasibility in terms of the required resources of time, finances and people being readily available and with the appropriate skills. The search for perfect solutions may be misguided. However, the belief in 'one best way' has a long history not just in management theory but also in more general considerations of how society might be organized. The philosopher Karl Popper (1966) used the phrase 'Utopian social engineering' to describe attempts to remodel society in accordance with some grand social plan. In contrast to this approach, Popper in his attack on Utopianism and dogma, argued for 'piecemeal social engineering' where change is brought about by social adjustments and readjustments which can be continually improved upon. However, the search for perfection has not lessened in attraction despite the apparent lack of success.

The managerial focus

Changes at the level of politics, social life, economics, ideas, and their impact upon organizations in terms of structures, people, tasks or processes have human costs and implications in terms of how people relate to each other and carry out their roles. We will be concerned with issues at the organizational and societal level such as how can the public interest be defined or what is the relationship between organizations and the wider community? However, we will investigate these macro issues via a more localized context through which the 'big' issues are given a focus. Localized issues are seen in terms of how they affect individuals and their relationships with each other. It is at this level that the manager can make sense of them. The macro issues are often general and value laden, often with a political overtone. 'Is the state the best guarantor of social justice?' might be a typical question raised at this macro and abstract level. Theory is played out at the micro level. There is no use speculating about ideals without some understanding of the issues for managers in their face-to-face activities. We will seek to locate the discussion at different levels. We also need to be clear about what sort of question we are dealing with – is it a technical question, a political one, a legal one or an ethical one? What distinguishes an ethical question from these other types of question? The manager faces all of these questions on a day-to-day basis. What are the key concerns of ethics and what are the key concerns of managers managing in a complex environment? The two questions need to be seen together, and some of the key issues are:

- Where is the balance to be maintained in practice between control and autonomy?
- What are the environmental constraints within which public services managers operate?
- How can public services managers internalize ethics?
- How can managers operate in an increasingly complex and ambiguous environment?
- How can individual values be reconciled with organizational values?
- How can public policy be best implemented so that it does not affect in an adverse way the recipients or users of the service?

Regime values

A key proposition investigated throughout this book is that ethical issues will always feature because of the nature of the public sector. The public sector is the place where political, social and economic values are located. It is concerned with how government treats its citizens. From Confucius onwards, it has been a key proposition that government is concerned with the welfare of the common people. How and by whom the common good is decided, and what it consists of, has always been the stuff of political debate. This view is expressed clearly by Ranson and Stewart (1994: 153):

'Public management is designed to serve the purposes of collective choice. In public organisations, activities are carried out to maintain and sustain ways of life, but also to enable change in society through response and development. Through these activities values are realised in the public domain.'

Stewart and Ranson (1988) argue that the purposes of the public sector distinguish it from the private sector. That there are fundamental differences between the two sectors has been contested. In a well-worn debate that continues to run and run, Mintzberg (1996) adds his considerable voice to those who argue that government should not be treated as a business. Protagonists in the debate have been characterized as either 'genericists' or 'differentialists' depending upon their belief either that management in the public sector is essentially the same as in the private sector or that there are fundamental differences between the two. Murray (1975), for example, argues that the two sectors are converging since a concern with efficiency or planning is a feature of management generally and that business is not just about profit and is constrained by a political and legal context. Rainey *et al.* (1976) and Stewart and Ranson (1988) take the opposite view and the latter argue that the purposes, conditions and tasks of the public sector are totally different to the private sector. Allison (1983) argues that public and private sector organizations are alike but in unimportant or superficial respects and that the conditions and content of the public sector are so different that the transfer of generic management skills is inappropriate. The debate is usually conducted in terms of:

- the goals or purposes of public and private sector organizations;
- the conditions within which they operate in terms of the political, social and economic environment;
- the functions that they perform;
- the processes, structures and techniques they adopt to achieve their goals;
- the people they employ and the skills they require.

However, any debate that relies upon a view that the public sector and the private sector can be treated as homogeneous entities will prove, ultimately, to be sterile. The diverse purposes of the public sector mean that different public services organizations will adopt different techniques and structures to carry out their functions and will charge for some functions, but not for others. Equally diverse is the private sector, in that there will be variations in ownership and management, size, structure, or functions. Mintzberg (1996) argues that the concept of the private sector used in the debate is too narrow and he distinguishes between organizations that are privately owned, publicly owned, state owned, cooperatively owned and 'non-owned' such as quangos.

Unfortunately this diversity has not been recognized by politicians, particularly in the UK, where the conventional wisdom among Conservative politicians has been that the private sector is by definition good and the public sector bad. This view is not unusual, nor confined to the UK; in his defence of bureaucracy in the USA, Goodsell (1994: 14) argues that bureaucracy is generally depicted, at least among some commentators, as '. . . inherently rigid, incapable of innovation, and riddled with fighting cliques and scheming careerists' and is characterized as 'oppressive, dangerous and despotic', and yet as Godsell argues, 'Most citizens are satisfied with their personal experiences with bureaucracy most of the time' (p. 29).

This book draws upon research carried out in a wide range of public services organizations and, where appropriate, private sector organizations. However, the nature of public service is sometimes implied, often unclear and frequently ambiguous. It is becoming even more so with the advocacy of partnerships between the public and private sectors, the fragmentation of service delivery and the growth in private welfare and security services. The activities of government have been justified on economic grounds as an alternative to markets in the allocation of resources and the provision of public goods, on political grounds concerning the upholding of sovereignty, and on social welfare grounds based upon some notion of common welfare and need. There are familiar arguments, on economic grounds, concerning a minimal role for the state, and they are described in Box 1.1.

The economic model of the state is built upon certain assumptions and is not a given; increasingly the private sector does supply public goods such as security, for example. Issues are raised concerning assumptions about the scope, nature and limits of state activity. However, irrespective of its scope those working within the public services are still faced with delivering services determined by political will, expressing political values, and which in some ways must be directed towards the common welfare, however defined. Political philosophy, from Plato's *Republic* onwards has been concerned with the justification for, and the limits of, the role of government. This role has been seen as having a legal, social, or economic character and its limits have ranged from the minimalist state, presiding over competing interests to the planned state, pursuing interventionist policies (see Downie 1964). Individual managers want to know what action to take or refrain from in certain circumstances; they want to feel confident that their actions are not causing harm and that they are 'doing well while doing good'. This is linked to some notion of what is, and what should be, the task of the manager. Is it to deliver services equitably, efficiently, effectively, to the best of their ability? How do we evaluate how well the manager is doing? This is a pertinent question as managers are expected to become more accountable for their actions. Vice President of the USA, Al Gore, has argued that a major impetus for change in the management of

Box 1.1 Classical economic rationale for government intervention

Classical economic analysis provides an account of why the state could provide certain types of goods and services. It is argued that markets, left to themselves, may produce too much of some goods but not enough of others. In the extreme case the market may fail altogether because of:

- the existence of externalities;
- the existence of public goods;
- imperfect competition;
- incomplete information;
- uncertainty.

Governments might intervene to correct market failure by regulating market exchanges, by policies which seek to stabilize market swings or by regulations which seek to prevent unfair competition. The existence of externalities and public goods may also prompt government intervention.

Externalities
An externality occurs when the consumption or production activities of one organization affect the welfare of others in a way that is not reflected in market prices. For example, an external cost arises from a smokey factory chimney which affects those that involuntarily consume the pollution. The social costs of production are the sum of the costs to the producer of inputs plus the costs to the third party of the externality. In the same way, external benefits and social benefits also occur. The existence of externalities generates costs and benefits that are not included in market prices. Governments can intervene to correct for market failure. For example, governments can impose pollution taxes or emission standards.

Collective goods
A further dimension to externalities is the existence of goods which yield benefits from which people cannot be excluded. Examples include defence and law and order. Such 'pure' public goods are usually supplied by the public sector. These goods can, however, be contracted out to the private sector. Whether or not to contract out these goods is, of course, subject to political debate.

There are other goods which are held in common ownership such as common land, and the air and sea where property rights are not assigned to individual owners. Like public goods these goods are said to be *non-excludable*, in contrast to private goods such as food or clothing from which people can be excluded unless they pay.

Pure public goods are also *non-rivalrous* in character. This means that the addition of another consumer will not lead to a subtraction from any other individual's consumption of that good. Defence has this characteristic. Common land, however, is rivalrous in consumption since one individual's use of it may be in competition with another individual's use. Here the government may intervene to limit the use of the resource so as to preserve the resource for common use.

Given the character of non-excludability, there is no incentive for a profit-seeking firm to provide the good since individuals cannot be excluded. People can obtain the benefits of public goods without paying for them. Collective provision by government can be paid for by taxing everybody. (See Open University 1993.)

the public services has come from a new understanding of how best to use human capital by pushing responsibility downwards (see Gore 1994). One criterion may be financial in nature and we can use criteria of efficiency and effectiveness or, increasingly, environmental friendliness. What does it mean to use ethics as another 'E'? Stewart (1989) has argued that the management of equity is crucial in the local government context, such that a perspective based upon the management of equity may involve:

- Developing marketing approaches to identify need rather than demand, and to discourage demands from those with fewer needs.
- An empirical analysis of which groups actually use, and benefit, from services.
- An analysis of the distribution of resources between different locations.
- An analysis of who are the winners and losers from policies.
- An analysis of the barriers to access to services for different groups and the introduction of assistance for those groups whose voices are rarely heard.
- A right to be heard for those individuals or groups who feel that they have been treated unfairly.

In examining the manager's task we are interested in how a task is done as well as what is done. At the same time, however, we need to consider how the concept of ethics is viewed by managers themselves. If ethics is seen as just an 'optional extra', expressed in the same way that an economic or a financial point of view can be expressed then inevitably the ethical perspective will not have much of a champion as managers are driven by the day-to-day considerations of their role. Chapter 7 examines the concept of 'doing well while doing good' by looking at how we evaluate managerial and organizational performance from the ethical point of view.

Conclusion

Individuals engage in a range of relationships located within a set of organizational and societal practices. A key question in understanding ethics and public services management is not just 'Is the manager ethical?' but, 'Has the organizational context changed so that the manager is more likely to make a mistake or be less liable to corruption, be less committed, be less professional and so on?' Is there more or less incentive to be corrupt or act unethically? Thus, we need to ask, not has the public service ethos declined, but what are the kinds of activities that the manager in the public services is now being asked to do and under what circumstances?

We can ask 'Why should managers be ethical?' but a better question might be 'Under what circumstances should managers refrain from, or carry out, an action on ethical grounds?' A number of considerations spring to mind in terms of individual conscience versus loyalty to the organization or codes of conduct and rules versus informal conventions and peer pressure. We can ask what is it that regulates behaviour? Is it orders, practices, conscience as a sense of duty, codes of conduct, peer groups, society generally, professional norms and standards of conduct, the law, or accounting standards? How is particular behaviour enforced? Can we condemn the individual manager who goes along with 'the way in which we do things around here' or supports the notion 'don't dob on your mates' (i.e. whistleblowing)?

At the heart of the discussion is the question of 'What does an ethical issue, decision or dilemma look like?' Are such dilemmas just the big issues in terms of fraud and corruption or are they also about how we treat others as human beings within an organizational context? Chapter 5 examines a number of relationships between the manager and a range of stakeholders in terms of rights, duties, obligations, loyalty and so on and examines the form that these relationships take as principal-agency relationships, contractual and quasi-market relationships, and professional-client relationships. We explore the understanding that ethics and public services management are best developed through an examination of the mode of relationship that public services managers operate through and with.

Thus, dealing with a citizen a client or a customer are three very different activities and involve different sorts of relationships which need to be recognized. The language of citizenship is that of, on the one hand, general rights, but on the other, fraternity and solidarity. The consumer is concerned with purchasing power, protected by a legal system providing consumer protection and rights. Clients will be interested in ensuring that they receive their entitlements and that their interests are protected.

We will examine seven propositions which capture the main issues in managing ethically in the public services:

1 The public service ethos is not generic but is given different meanings depending upon relationships and context.
2 Codes of conduct are necessary but not sufficient in regulating behaviour.
3 In undermining professionalism we have thrown out the baby with the bathwater.
4 The ultimate goal of government is the welfare of the common people (after Aristotle).
5 It is not managers themselves who are inherently dishonest but the institutional context within which they operate.
6 Issues are often not clear-cut and will change over time and between places.
7 How services are delivered is as important as what is delivered.

Any discussion of ethics takes place upon shifting sands. What is to count as ethical behaviour will also change over time and between places.

This truism has led some commentators to argue that we cannot say anything significant about ethics because of ethical relativism and subjectivity. Such arguments take the form of 'It depends upon the circumstances' or 'You have to take account of the context' or 'You have to understand their beliefs and values and not impose your own judgements'. All of this is true, of course, and it is difficult to justify universal principles when we accept that, under certain circumstances, lying can be justified and that rules can be broken. Different accounts of ethical principles are discussed in Chapter 3, and in anticipation of those discussions we need a working definition of ethics and morals. For the most part, the two terms are used interchangeably. However, this book will distinguish between:

1 **Ethics** as a set of principles, often defined as a code that acts as a guide to conduct. This set of principles provides a framework for acting.
2 **Morals** as concerned with action, with how a person lives up to the demands of what is perceived to be right action. Thus, an individual may be aware of ethical principles and still act immorally. This is developed further in Chapter 3.

Two further considerations relevant to the public services manager are, first, what if discretion was widespread and the only basis for decisions? It may be argued that rule-following can be inflexible, that rules cannot cover every contingency, that rules do not allow the exercise of judgement. However, discretion assumes that decision-makers are competent and do not act in their own interest but act to further the interests of their clients.

Second, what if we could not rely on individuals or governments to fulfil their promises? Obligations would not be willingly undertaken, enforcement would be rife, there would be no trust or social relations. It might be an impoverished life but it might work through the use of contracts. Even contracts need to be located within a social practice of trust otherwise why not just break the contract? Denhardt (1988: 100) considers that: 'The ethical administrator is one who examines in a critical and independent manner the standards by which decisions are made, attempting to reflect the morality of society as well as acting in consideration of the administrator's commitments, obligations and responsibilities to the organisation and to other individuals and groups to whom the administrator is accountable'.

This book seeks to clarify some of the issues and reflect upon the commitments, obligations and responsibilities that public services managers have to a range of stakeholders.

two

Ethical issues

Key issues

- The nature of ethical issues as perceived by different stakeholders.
- The range of issues that might face the public services manager.
- The location of issues at the social, organizational and individual levels.

Introduction

Chapter 1 indicated that ethical issues can be located at different levels: the individual, the organizational and the social levels. It also introduced the notion that ethics can be seen at a macro and a micro level. This chapter will examine the notion of ethical issues in further detail by addressing a number of questions:

- What is the issue?
- What makes it an issue?
- What makes it an ethical issue?
- For whom is it an issue?
- Who defines it as an issue?
- At what level is it an issue – social, organizational or individual?

In simple terms, issues are raised because of a disagreement over an important topic of discussion or action. What is important may be open to question and this may be reflected in the ease with which issues are re-solved. Difficulties will arise in identifying issues since it may be impossible in advance to predict which topics or proposed courses of action will lead to disagreement. A further problem may arise, in the context of public services, where proposed courses of action may be legal but may have unethical consequences.

'In deciding whether a particular action is ethical, public servants should consider whether the impact of the decision will be fair, whether the action is guided by responsiveness to the needs of the community and the government, whether they would be happy to have the action made public, and whether they could easily justify the action if called on to do so' (Management Advisory Board 1996). This statement raises a number of questions concerning the values of openness, fairness, needs and responsiveness. It is also concerned with doing the right thing, with an action that can be justified. There may be occasions when we think that an action has nothing to do with morals or do not consider it to raise any issues. There is a range of questions that form part of the continuing debate concerning the roles and responsibilities of public services managers to which we now turn our attention and these appear to be universal in scope.

Issues enduring and universal

Chapter 1 referred to the investigation into sleaze in the UK. The UK is not the only country faced with corruption.

Similar issues to those highlighted in Box 2.1 can be found elsewhere. For example, the Australian Independent Commission Against Corruption

---

Box 2.1 Sleaze seeps out of gift wrapping – Jonathan Watts

It is open season for corruption in Japan again. For the past month newspapers have been full of stories about bureaucrats on the take, politicians receiving illegal donations, doctors being paid to falsify research and police accepting bribes . . . The main target of the latest purge has been the former chief civil servant at the ministry of health and welfare, Nobuharu Okamitsu . . . The police allege that Mr Okamitsu took a kickback of 60 million yen (£310,000) after granting state subsidies to a nursing home contractor. Another ministry official has been arrested, one sacked and 15 others punished for accepting expensive meals, golf club memberships and cash gifts from the same source . . . 'The shocking thing is that nobody is shocked anymore,' said Professor Takeshi Sasaki . . . 'Many Japanese, including myself, suspect that this kind of thing is going on all the time. Okamitsu's case and the others merely confirm our suspicions: corruption is an everyday phenomenon.' One reason the problem is so pervasive, said Professor Sasaki, is Japan's gift-giving culture. 'It is very difficult to distinguish between a gift and a bribe and this complicates the situation immensely.'

(Edited extract from the *Guardian* newspaper, 23 December 1996)

(ICAC 1991) looked at 19 key areas in its first two years, grouped under four main headings: dealings between public and private sector, election funding and contributions to party coffers, managing performance and internal audit, and a range of 'others'. The 19 issues were concerned with:

- No free lunches – meals received by police while on duty.
- Currying favour with officialdom.
- Tendering.
- Relations with the private sector.
- Letting contracts.
- Outside employment.
- Involvement of ministers in day-to-day matters.
- Internal audit.
- Accountability.
- Use of codes of conduct.
- 'Dobbing on mates' i.e. whistleblowing.

In its more recent bulletin *Corruption Matters* (ICAC 1997) the ICAC examined:

- Loyalty and personal integrity and the possible clash between the two.
- A local government building inspector accused of taking bribes from a developer.
- The operation of Aboriginal land councils.
- Embezzlement.
- Conflicts of interest.
- Codes of conduct and the relationship between police and criminals.
- Corruption.
- Work environment as a threat to integrity.

In the USA the 'revolving door' between the public and private sector has long been a concern. The concept refers to relationships between commercial firms bidding for multi-million pound contracts and the public officials responsible for awarding the contracts. Such relationships are fostered by inside knowledge and 'top drawer' contacts. In the USA it is blatant, with high-level officials switching jobs from presidential adviser on arms control to a post with a missile manufacturer and back again to rejoin the Pentagon. Regulations can be imposed such that it is forbidden to take up a private sector post until a time period has elapsed. Thus, it is illegal in the USA to take up a comparable job in the private sector after leaving public service until two years have elapsed. It is arguable whether such restrictions in effect act as a 'restraint on trade' by forbidding former civil servants from taking full advantage of their knowledge and expertise. In the USA, the practice became known as the 'iron triangle' – the mutually sustaining links between officials, consultants and private defence contractors which, it has been argued, can lead to waste and extravagant arms build-up. In the UK the *Guardian* newspaper of 25 January 1995 reported that more than 2000 Ministry of Defence civil servants and armed forces personnel have joined British and foreign defence companies and management consultants in the past decade. In a similar fashion BUPA, the private healthcare company appointed Sir Duncan Nichol (former Chief Executive of the NHS Management Executive) to a senior position 18 months after he left his job with detailed knowledge of the NHS. Why is this an issue? Only if he received preferential treatment from old colleagues?

The research carried out by the OECD (1996) seems to indicate that, despite differences between different countries, there is a growing convergence in terms of a concern that fundamental values associated with public services organizations are being undermined by the reforms, outlined in Chapter 1, that have taken place. The report argues that some of these 'adjustments' '. . . may have had unintended impacts on ethics and standards of conduct' (p. 26).

These impacts can be broadly summarized as follows:

- Working with limited resources may affect morale as managers may be less willing to give that bit extra. Although the report argues that there is not much evidence that people succumb to outright bribery, when cost-cutting takes place training may be the first to go and outside employment may be more attractive. The report also identified post-employment restrictions as discussed above.
- Citizen demands can lead to a conflict between client rights and the obligation to keep within economic limits. Managers will need to balance public interests against customers' interests.
- Restructuring and the fragmentation into business units and cost centres may well mean that Civil Service norms disappear, raising concerns over accountability and responsibility.
- A devolved and discretionary management environment may lead to the erosion of a service-wide ethic.
- An increase in managerial discretion may lead managers to take risks, increasing the possibility of mistakes; there may be less supervision at central levels; trade-offs between efficiency and ethics may occur.
- The public-private interface, such that direct contact is increased, may lead to greater temptation to treat contractors favourably as illustrated in the 'revolving door' issue.
- Working in a fishbowl of open scrutiny where the 'faceless bureaucrat' is a being from the past.
- The move to short-term contracts and decentralized decision-making has created a climate in which ethical issues are more subtle and likely to arise at a lower level within the organization.

- Changing social norms.
- A changing international environment.

Many of the above have the status of conjecture and in later chapters and in the sections that follow we examine the evidence for such statements. Whatever their status, there is the perception that a range of issues have appeared on the agenda as a result of developments and reforms in the management of public services worldwide.

The UK experience

In a recent report from the Audit Commission (1996b) on probity in local government, a crackdown on fraud carried out by the Audit Commission led to a significant increase in the amount of fraud identified from £46.5 million in 1994/5 to £69.5 million in 1995/6. 166,000 fraud cases were detected in 1995/6, an increase of 48 per cent on the previous year. The Audit Commission pointed out that only 1 per cent of the total amount of fraud resulted from proven fraud by local government staff and 99 per cent was perpetrated against local government. Benefits fraud is the biggest area. Some of the rise is due to improved detection rates.

According to the Audit Commission report, the number of proven cases of corruption in local government is low. In 1995/6 the number dropped to its lowest level since 1990/1 when the Commission began recording

---

Box 2.2 Examples of fraud perpetrated by local government officers

Case study 1
A clerk stole £120,000 by generating fraudulent invoices of overpaid business rates. The clerk used a supervisor's computer password to change the names and addresses of companies with large credit balances, initiated refund forms and arranged for the refunds to be passed to her. She then paid the cheques into bank accounts that she had opened for the purpose. The fraud was discovered when the supervisor checked a refund of £28,000 and found it to be fraudulent.

Case study 2
A housing maintenance officer submitted false invoices in respect of two renovation grants. The officer created a bogus list of works to be done and submitted false invoices from a fictitious contractor with a non-existent VAT registration number. The contractor who actually carried out the works submitted invoices directly to the officer for amounts significantly less than the value of those paid by the authority. The defaulter processed the payments himself. The total value of the fraudulent payments was £23,000.

Source: Audit Commission 1996b

Table 2.1 Corruption: trend analysis

Case type	[Number of cases]					
	1990/1	1991/2	1992/3	1993/4	1994/5	1995/6
Tendering, award and settlement of contracts	12	15	20	15	15	11
Award of permissions, planning consents, licenses, allocations, grants and loans	4	9	9	6	15	4
Disposal of assets	3	4	3	0	3	2
Other (including canvassing, pressure selling and non-disclosure of interests)	19	23	22	15	24	4
Total number of cases	**38**	**51**	**54**	**36**	**57**	**21**

Source: Audit Commission 1996b: 7.

data (see Table 2.1). The report recognized the problems associated with coordinating the activities of the different organizations that might be responsible for the allocation of the various benefits. The ethical implications may lie in the extent to which organizations put pressure on their staff to act illegally.

The Audit Commission also carried out a similar report concerned with the NHS (Audit Commission 1996a), *Protecting the Public Purse: Ensuring Probity in the NHS (1996 Update)*. Auditors expressed a concern that management had still not accepted prime responsibility '. . . for putting in place strong systems of control that prevent and detect fraud and corruption and which encourage an anti-fraud culture throughout the NHS' (p. 4). The report found that the biggest area of fraud within the NHS is prescriptions which has been estimated to cost the NHS between £30 million and £69 million per year.

Case study

Over a period of several years, a dispensing GP in a rural practice issued bogus prescriptions in the names of patients at a residential home for the elderly. Investigations revealed that the patients had not received the treatments and, in two cases, prescriptions had been issued for patients who had been dead for over a year (the GP had himself issued their death certificates). The total value of prescriptions for treatments not supplied but claimed for over a period of five years exceeded £700,000.

Source: Audit Commission 1996a: 8.

The Audit Commission report (1996a: 14) highlights the process issues:

NHS trust and HA [health authority] boards and senior managers must remain vigilant and ensure that a strong framework of effective internal controls is in place to prevent and detect fraud and corruption. The majority of fraud cases occur in areas of lax controls, poor segregation of duties and lack of regular monitoring. This fact reinforces the need for management to review constantly the effectiveness of their control arrangements.

The regulation of behaviour is revisited in Chapter 5 where we discuss the success of regulating behaviour by codes of conduct versus the internalization of values.

The Committee of Public Accounts has been at the heart of the debate concerning the ethical dimension to the activities of public officials (see Committee of Public Accounts 1994). The report found examples of the following failures and inadequacies.

Failures of inadequate financial controls

The report found evidence of: inadequate internal accounting control systems; inexperienced staff lacking financial training and expertise; failure to pursue money owed; paying bills without checking invoices and poor monitoring of capital expenditure. For example, it was found that the Department of Employment had difficulties in controlling and monitoring expenditure on the Technical and Vocational Education Initiative (TVEI). This initiative aimed to influence state education in ways which prepare 14–18-year-olds better for working life. The department accepted that their regional offices had lacked the financial expertise to manage their budgets effectively. Similar criticism had been levelled against it before in its failure to financially manage the employment training and youth training programmes. A key issue is, therefore, a failure of organizations to adequately prepare staff for changes in devolved budgeting. Such lack of preparation may put undue stress on individuals and it is, therefore, not the individuals at fault but the department.

Other departments included under the inadequate financial control heading were:

- Foreign and Commonwealth Office
- Property Service Agency Services
- Insolvency Service of the Department of Trade and Industry
- Ministry of Defence
- Department of Social Security
- Wessex Regional Health Authority
- National Rivers Authority

The failure to impose adequate financial controls is not therefore unique.

Failure to comply with rules

The report found: *ex gratia* payments made on termination of contract without authorization; payments of grants without evidence of entitlement; failure to secure full recovery of benefits to senior executives to which they were not entitled. The departments cited as being at fault included the Department of Employment, the Welsh Development Agency and the West Midlands Regional Health Authority (WMRHA).

For example, the director of regionally managed services of the WMRHA was allowed to leave on redundancy terms after five years' service with an immediate pension of £6462 per year and lump sums totalling £81,837. The authority and the NHS management executive subsequently told the Committee of Public Accounts that he should have been dismissed, not made redundant. The WMRHA argued that it did not previously possess the full facts, indicating a failure to know about and control what senior staff were doing in its name.

Inadequate stewardship of public money and assets

The report cited examples of: inadequate oversight by those in authority; failure to establish effective controls over non-departmental bodies; failure to hold individuals to account; failure to establish clear lines of accountability; failure to take prompt corrective action. Departments quoted included: the Welsh Office; Wessex Regional Health Authority; WMRHA; Forward Civil Service Catering; and the Ministery of Defence.

For example, the NHS Management Executive (NHSME) was criticized regarding cost overruns and delays on the building of the Chelsea and Westminster Hospital. The report identified the need for full and proper financial planning before any commitment is made to future capital schemes.

Failure to provide value for money

The report found evidence of: conflicts of interest with private sector contractors; inadequate control over computer projects often embarked upon with inadequate information; inadequate management of major capital projects. The National Rivers Authority was cited for its mismanagement of its headquarters relocation, characterized by inadequate and poorly-controlled tendering and contracting arrangements, and attendant risks of fraud, corruption and failure to obtain value for money. Also cited in the report were the Wessex Regional Health Authority, several New Town Development Corporations and the Department of Employment.

The report argues that it is not so much the immoral behaviour of individual managers that is of concern but the failure of existing procedures and rules.

In his consideration of public sector changes and their ethical implications, Doig (1995) raises the question of whether the issues are transitional or have more fundamental causes. He argues that inquiries in the 1980s (into the Property Services Agency and the Crown Agents) focused on misconduct but also raised general areas of internal organizational or procedural weaknesses including:

> weak guidance on standards of conduct or non-compliance with procedures; management indifference or ignorance; inadequate financial and management information systems; lax working practices; poor staff relations; sub-organizational autonomy; no separation of functions; excessive discretion; inadequate recruitment, promotion and training policies; and crucially, the increasing contact with private sector values, personnel and practices which could result in the exploitation of weak public sector procedures and standards as well as persuading public officials of the acceptability of personal financial gain.
>
> (Doig 1995: 193)

To summarize, then, ethical concerns appear likely to arise because of:

- Immoral behaviour on the part of officials (an enduring feature and one which we examine below).
- Lack of skills in drawing-up contracts or monitoring performance.
- Proximity to the private sector.
- Access to a saleable commodity, e.g. prescriptions.
- Lack of controls.

These issues are located at the individual and the organizational levels.

Doig (1995) argues that many of the attempts to curb immoral behaviour constitute firefighting, in so far as such reforms tend to look at or deal with specific examples rather than the deep underlying causes. He argues that: '. . . public officials have been subject to a range of new influences, imperatives and objectives that appear to override normal standards of conduct' (p. 200), and these are concerned with: changes in personnel and their attitudes; agency independence which allows accountability to escape at arms-length; privatization and the commercialization of activities; information technology; the private delivery of public services; and changing political objectives. However, is the evidence that fraud or corruption has increased as a result of the changing landscape of public services management convincing? It may be that we are simply better at detecting fraud, as bodies such as the Audit Commission become more efficient or devote more resources to detection. In other words, perhaps the regulatory process has just become more efficient. It may be that a long-term solution is to improve ethics awareness through training. Doig suggests the vetting of recruits, the use of staff handbooks, training, risk and behaviour profiling,

separation of duties, rotation of staff, systems security, appropriate management and assurance checks, and investigation and disciplinary procedures.
The issue of training is examined in Chapter 8.

Managers' perspectives

Some of the issues identified above appear to be relatively straightforward,
particularly those where a law is broken; we can all recognize fraud and
corruption when we see it. Or can we? The ICAC in Australia carried out
a survey on corruption with more than 1300 New South Wales public
officials. The researchers used a number of scenarios to determine how corrupt behaviour was perceived and the findings indicated that individuals
hold different perceptions of what constitutes corruption. The scenarios
were the release of confidential information, use of office facilities, use of
government stationery, small Christmas gifts, using a position to get a job
for a friend, bypassing tendering processes because of the shortness of
time, and claiming travel expenses. The public officials took the view that
definitions of corruption depended upon:

- personal gain;
- breaking the rules – if no rules are broken then the action cannot be
  corrupt;
- how often it happens;
- the value of the gifts.

The context was deemed to be crucial as were considerations of whether
or not harm was caused to others. What may be illegal may not necessarily
be seen as immoral. Hetzner and Schmidt (1986) point up the dangers of
reducing morality to law and argue that moral conduct could be whatever
the courts said it was. They add:

> More often than reducing morality to law, however, public adminis-
> tration has substituted prudential or technical considerations for ethi-
> cal ones – one of the most notable methods being via cost-benefit
> calculation or risk assessment. For instance, cost-benefit analyses have
> been applied to environmental issues in such a way that the question,
> 'What is good for Society?' is answered as if the question were, 'What
> is efficient for Society?' The point to be made here is not that consid-
> erations of efficiency are not important in environmental policy or
> should not figure in our ethical deliberations but rather that efficiency
> calculations are not necessarily synonymous with or substitutable for
> moral ones.

(p. 435)

Definitions of what is to count as corrupt or unethical behaviour are not clear-cut and, not only that, but managers asked to respond to ethics-type questionnaires will be reluctant to admit to any unethical behaviour unless, of course, complete anonymity can be preserved! Consider the questionnaire presented in Box 2.3. What answers would you give?

Box 2.3 Questionnaire: ethics at work

Please tick the appropriate column	Never	Sometimes	Often
1 Have you taken stationery or other minor items home from your workplace for personal use?			
2 Have you used the office telephone for personal calls?			
3 Have you asked a colleague to say you are not in when you are?			
4 Have you told 'white lies' to customers or clients along the lines of 'the cheque is in the post' when it is not?			
5 Have you blamed your subordinates?			
6 Have you criticized your organization to outsiders?			
7 Have you exaggerated your achievements?			
8 Have you revealed confidential information about individuals to others?			
9 Have you done what you believed to be wrong because everyone else does it?			
10 Have you tempered advice to politicians/ senior managers to give them what they want to hear?			
11 Have you taken free lunches from clients or customers?			
12 Have you shifted blame for your mistakes to others elsewhere in the organization, e.g. its 'head office's fault'?			
13 Have you bent the rules to get things done?			
14 Have you carried out a task that you fundamentally disagreed with?			
15 Have you covered up for a colleague?			

	Never	Sometimes	Often
16 Have you acted in favour of a contractor or client because of a bribe?			
17 Have you acted in favour of a contractor or client out of friendship?			
18 Have you accepted hospitality, over and above that prescribed in codes of conduct?			
19 Have you discriminated against potential or existing staff on the basis of age, colour, sexual orientation, gender, religion, race?			
20 Have you presented misleading information?			
21 Have you manipulated performance indicators so as to reach targets?			
22 Have you kept information back from clients concerning entitlements because of resource constraints?			

Did you answer 'never' to all the questions? The point of the exercise, however, is not to demonstrate how 'squeaky clean' you are but to show the vast range of choices that we face in our organizational lives. All the questions in Box 2.3 seem to involve:

- our relationships with others, both inside and outside organizations;
- our relationships with the organization as a whole;
- values;
- our personal behaviour;
- the relationship between means and ends;
- stealing;
- fraud;
- loyalty;
- impartiality.

How you responded will demonstrate how you perceive organizational behaviour. We are not here to indicate 'right' and 'wrong' behaviour but to indicate where ethical considerations might come into play. Cultural relativities will feature; for example, it is perfectly acceptable in certain parts of the world to award jobs on the basis of family ties, and it is considered wrong not to do so. It is a mistake to assume that all ethical issues can be located within the categories of fraud or corruption even though this has tended to be the major focus of those who have tried to legislate ethics. This does beg the question that ethical issues are those which can be legislated for and raises the question of what is moral behaviour.

Table 2.2 OUBS research

Do you believe that your organization encourages you to:	Never (%)	Sometimes (%)	Often (%)
Take risks	15	70	15
Act unlawfully	80	15	5
Act unethically	61	34	5
Take short cuts	11	61	28
Abide by the rules	8	17	75
Treat different clients differently	10	61	29
Misrepresent performance	29	60	11
Massage statistics	24	57	19
Get involved in the running of the organization	5	49	46
Treat colleagues and subordinates badly	54	35	11
Make best use of your skills	10	49	41
Recognize the contributions of others	11	41	48

Most of the issues seem to be fairly mundane but they are concerned with the activities of public officials which include policy advice, regulating other agencies, meeting targets, delivering services, raising revenue and so on. Most managers take part in activities that could involve moral decisions. Apart from the issues that might arise because of individual perceptions of moral behaviour, there are others that arise from the organizational context within which individuals work. In research carried out with a group of 45 Open University Business School (OUBS) MBA students who are middle and senior managers drawn from across the public services in the UK (including those working in local government, central government, the health service, education, the voluntary sector and the armed forces) 12 key issues were raised and the results are shown in Table 2.2.

The ethical focus is on the relationship between the manager and the organization and the expectations that are generated. We illustrate some of the issues by examining a MORI poll carried out on behalf of the Association of First Division Civil Servants, the trade union for senior officials within the UK Civil Service, between July and September 1996 (MORI 1996). The poll was directed at those in the Crown Prosecution Service (CPS), 1347 questionnaires were distributed and the response rate was 58 per cent (786). The overwhelming number of respondents were lawyers, who reported that their dedication to public service and their professionalism are under threat. A certain level of cynicism was expressed about how the organization perceives its staff. Respondents were asked to compare the characteristics of colleagues who they felt were worthy of progress with the criteria that the respondents felt were, in fact, recognized by the organization (see Table 2.3).

Table 2.3 Response of the CPS to 1996 MORI poll

Characteristic	Ideal (%)	Actual (%)
High level of professional skills	99	18
Is open and frank	90	5
Prepared to raise issues concerning professional principles	74	4
Committed to the public service	72	19
Actively looks for promotion	13	73
Toes the line	1	92
Uses intimidation	1	43
Is secretive	0	57
Is dishonest	0	24

Source: adapted from MORI 1996.

A number of explanations were offered by the respondents for their disillusionment with their organization including:

- 79 per cent said that they had too much work to do.
- Many argued that their legal expertise was not sufficiently recognized.
- They were expected to spend too much time on administration and not enough on legal work.
- Career expectations were not fulfilled.
- They felt poorly informed about what was going on in the organization.
- They did not believe that senior management responded to or took seriously staff views.
- They believed that the service was being run down for political reasons.

The findings raise disturbing questions concerning the relationship between the employer and the employee and lead to concerns about the types of organization that exist in the public sector. One view of a local authority, for example, is to see the organization as a community through which relationships are played out and which shares a common purpose. Another view sees the organization at the centre of a web of contractual relationships, buying in expertise when required. Clearly, different relationships will obtain depending upon how those relationships are perceived and mirrored in terms of organizational goals and structures.

Apart from the general considerations that managers will have concerning their role, there may well be more specific considerations arising from their professional and occupational roles. Danley *et al.* (1996) carried out a survey among human resource (HR) professionals in the USA and identified a range of possible HR practices that may have ethical dimensions. These included: recruitment, training, compensation, rewards, promotion, job assignment, discipline, termination of contracts and recruitment. Out of the 37 issues that they identified, only seven were judged serious by more than a quarter of their 1078 respondents. These were:

1 Hiring, training or promotion based upon favouritism (30.7%).
2 Allowing differences in pay, discipline, promotion etc. due to friendships with top management (30.7%).
3 Sexual harassment (28.4%).
4 Sex discrimination in promotion (26.9%).
5 Using discipline for managerial and non-managerial personnel inconsistently (26.9%).
6 Not maintaining confidentiality (26.4%).
7 Sex discrimination on compensation (25.8%).

Danley *et al.* (1996) found that there were a number of key factors that influenced unethical behaviour and these included: the attitudes and behaviour of senior management; the attitudes and behaviour of supervisors; performance pressures; internal and external competition; pressures from friends and co-workers; lack of standards within the profession; lack of legislation; and personal values. We must question the extent to which it is individual shortcomings that lead to unethical behaviour. The organizational culture, the organizational processes and the attitudes of colleagues all go to make up the ethical fabric of an organization as much as the nature of its business or the moral behaviour of individuals. Badaracco and Webb (1995), in their research involving 30 recent MBA graduates of Harvard University, found that there were four powerful organizational 'commandments' that encouraged unethical behaviour, and organizational pressures rather than character flaws appeared to be the crucial factor:

1 Performance is what really counts – targets must be met.
2 Be loyal and show that you are a team player.
3 Don't break the law.
4 Don't over-invest in ethical behaviour.

In their research, Steinberg and Austen (1990) presented 1000 US government officials with a set of 14 ethical dilemmas and the following reasons were given to justify unethical behaviour:

- Good intentions – managers expressed frustration with red tape and took short cuts to achieve what they believed to be desirable ends.
- Ego 'power-trip'.
- Plain greed.
- Ignorance of rules, laws, codes, policies and procedures.
- It comes with the territory.
- Friendship.
- Ideology.
- Personal or family gain.

- Post-employment 'revolving door'.
- Financial problems and pressures.
- Stupidity.
- Exploiting the exploiters – a feeling of being hard done by and getting one's own back.
- Playing games.
- Going along with the norms, not making waves.
- Survival at all costs.
- Following orders.

We examine the relationship between the individual and the organization in more detail in Chapter 6 and we examine the implications of performance evaluation for ethics in Chapter 7.

Conclusion

This chapter has tried to demonstrate that issues arise within organizations which have an ethical dimension to them even though there will be disagreement concerning what to include. However, the research illustrated above, and drawn from different types of organization, seems to indicate that such issues will arise at several levels: the individual, the organizational and the social and each has implications for the way in which people are regarded and the way human resources are managed. MacLagan (1995: 161–2) makes the point that:

> The emphasis on decison-making in 'dramatic' cases which is so often assumed to be the essence of business ethics, deflects attention from the point that, since many ethical issues are much more pervasive than that, these may be overlooked. The everyday things – matters of discourse and conduct towards others . . . or the insidious way in which systemic factors such as culture, control mechanisms and 'taken-for-granted' culture in the organisation . . . can have ethical implications – need to be brought to people's attention.

This is the position taken throughout this book. We need to consider what are the general implications for public services managers and what are the specific issues arising as a result of performing a particular role within the public services. Much of the research carried out, as illustrated above, focuses upon moral dilemmas for managers. There are also ethical issues that will arise for the users of the services provided. Most definitions of ethics, to which we turn to in the next chapter, involve some notion of the effects of an individual's actions on others. Many of the issues raised are concerned with how managers treat a range of different stakeholders in terms of obligations, duties and rights and such concepts are at the heart of theorizing about ethics. Such obligations, for those working in the public services, are said to arise because of their positions of trust, power and privilege and the resulting obligation not to breach that trust, misuse that power or abuse that privilege. Many of the issues discussed above do appear to be enduring and are not found just in one part of the world. Part of the explanation lies in the fact that relations with employees, contractors, politicians or clients and customers are involved, and how we treat each other is of fundamental ethical concern.

At the same time organizational pressures and imperatives to meet targets, manage with scarce resources, and respond to a range of different stakeholders are not unique. Indeed, as the research reported above carried out by Badaracco and Webb (1995) indicates, such pressures are not even unique to public services organizations, as managers in the private sector face the same imperatives.

However, many of the issues discussed arise because of some deep underlying concerns about ethics which are reflected in concepts such as justice, rights, obligations, duties, etc. which in turn reflect some notion of right or wrong. Why do we consider something to be right or wrong? It must be because it is concerned with ethical principles which reflect and are reflected in societal and organizational practices. It is to a consideration of these ethical principles that we now turn.

three

Ethical theory and public service principles

Key issues

- Locating moral actions within an ethical framework.
- The role of ethical principles in guiding the actions of managers within organizations.
- Identifying those principles which characterize public administration and public services management.

Introduction and definitions

As we indicated in Chapter 1, practical guidance is grounded in theory, recognized in the concluding paragraphs of the economist J.M. Keynes's *The General Theory of Employment, Interest and Money* (1936: 383–4):

the ideas of economists and political philosophers, both when they are right and when they are wrong, are more powerful than is commonly understood. Indeed the world is ruled by little else. Madmen in authority, who hear voices in the air, are distilling their frenzy from some academic scribbler of a few years back. I am sure that the power of vested interests is vastly exaggerated compared with the gradual encroachment of ideas. Not, indeed, immediately, but after a certain interval; for in the field of economic and political philosophy there are not many who are influenced by new theories after they are twenty-five or thirty years of age, so that the ideas which civil servants and even agitators apply are not likely to be the newest. But, soon or late, it is ideas, not vested interests, which are dangerous for good and evil.

We are concerned with ethics as a practical guide rather than solely as a set of theories about human action. However, we do need a theoretical background. Ethics can be defined as a set of principles, often in turn defined as a code or system that acts as a guide to conduct. In simple terms, for example, the ethical code that has dominated Western thinking is based upon a mixture of Christian and humanist principles. Other ethical codes will reflect different religious and secular traditions. What they do have in common, however, is a concern with how individuals act, what their intentions are in so acting, and a set of values concerned with right and wrong action, however defined. These values will constitute more than a set of preferences. Respect for human life is a value that is significant; preference for a particular model of car may be a value but is not usually thought to be grounded in ethical principles. We could base the decision to buy a car on ethical grounds by insisting that we would not buy a car produced in a country that has a poor record of human rights (in May 1997, the new Labour government's foreign secretary, Robin Cook, has made it clear that British foreign policy on arms dealing would have an ethical dimension to it). Or we could insist on a car that has state-of-the-art safety features in order to protect ourselves and our passengers.

The relationship between values and ethics, particularly when doing business abroad is not clear-cut. You will recall that in Chapter 1 we examined the concept of cultural relativism where, for example, in Asia organizational values include loyalty, and honouring authority; in East India leadership at lower levels tends to be paternalistic and autocratic, and power sharing with subordinates and workers is viewed as a weakness; in Latin America the practice of handing out gratuities or bribes for getting something done is legal and an expected form of doing business. We have to be aware that different social groups and cultures have different ethical codes and that there may be no objective standard that can be used to judge one code to be better than another, that an ethical code is merely one among many, that there are no universal truths and that it is arrogant of us to assume that our way is the best way. Such arguments are powerful.

Despite this, values are beliefs that are deemed to be socially and personally desirable and are also recognized as being important in organizations. They can serve both an ethical function and a competence function. Thus, efficiency is a key organizational value which tells us more about the competence of an organization than its ethics. Within organizations, personal values may conflict with those held by the organization as a whole. The pursuit of achievement and ambition as a personal value may conflict with the organizational requirements relating to cooperation, and vice versa; increasingly college lecturers are encouraged to adopt competitive values and to retain students at all costs. This may conflict with personally held values concerning educational quality.

However, the notions of good and bad, right and wrong, are an essential part of moral language but their meaning is sometimes obscure. For example, is the good manager the same as the good person? But, you might say, who is to decide what is good and bad? This is at the heart of ethics theorizing. It is about individuals making decisions based upon perceptions concerning a range of issues involving other people and ourselves. As individuals with consciences who choose to engage in relations with others we need to work out how we will treat those individuals and how we would wish them to treat us. Presumably we can construct a list of criteria that are said to define the good manager and these will include notions of efficiency, effectiveness, loyalty, enthusiasm, commitment and resourcefulness. What would the criteria for the good person consist of? It might include being sensitive to the needs of others, respecting privacy and the rights of others, acting unselfishly and honestly, being loyal to family and friends etc. In asking the question what is the good manager or the good person we might also ask 'Is the same definition to be applied universally?'

We have also used the term 'moral' in the discussion. Following on from the definition offered in Chapter 1, we take morality to be concerned with action in the sense that an individual may have a firm grasp of the ethical principles at stake in a particular issue but decide to act immorally. Ethics is taken to be concerned with providing the framework for action, and morality is acting. After reading this book, for example, we cannot say 'Now, managers, go out there and be moral'. What we can do is provide a framework for understanding and evaluating managerial activity from an ethical perspective. From this perspective, morality is concerned with actions whereas ethics is more concerned with setting the boundaries for appropriate action. We can draw some boundaries around what are considered to be moral or immoral actions but we cannot tell you what to do! However, 'morals' defines how a person lives up to the demands of what is perceived to be correct behaviour. Ethics defines the effort to systemize and define the reasons for our moral assessments. We do pass judgements on our own and others' actions from an ethical point of view.

What are the kinds of judgement that can be made? Is making a moral decision similar to making any other kind of decision where we add up the pros and cons and proceed if the pros outweigh the cons? What are the principles that guide peoples' behaviour? Consider just a few:

- Act in accordance with rules.
- Act with a sense of justice, equality or freedom.
- Act so that whatever you do has the most beneficial consequences for the most people.
- Act out of a sense of virtue.
- Act in a way that satisfies your conscience.

- Act in a way that satisfies your desires or needs.
- Act in a way because everybody else acts in the same way.
- Act in a way because you are told to do so.

For example, a manager may be facing a decision on how to allocate an annual bonus. How to distribute rewards is a key task for many managers. The manager could consider one of four possible approaches:

1 To each person an equal share: this would ensure parity of rewards but does not recognize individual contribution and does not distinguish between those who have performed well and those who have performed indifferently.
2 To each person according to individual effort: this respects the effort that each person makes but, once again does not reward excellence or the quality of contribution.
3 To each person according to individual need: this would reward loyalty and recognizes the unique circumstances of individuals but it minimizes fairness to others and the pursuit of excellence and is based upon other factors not related to work.
4 To each person according to the usefulness of his or her contribution: this recognizes excellence but minimizes respect for everyone's individual skills and abilities and assumes that usefulness can be measured.

In education, as more and more team projects form part of the assessment strategy, one way of giving out individual marks is by allocating the team an overall mark and letting the team members decide how to distribute those marks on the basis of individual contribution.

However, in terms of definitions we also need to distinguish between values and principles. Too often values are dressed up as principles. A principle is a guide to action; a value is a preference expressed. We also need to be aware of actions undertaken by individuals *qua* individuals and individuals in the roles of managers and public services managers.

Theory

Chapter 1 indicated that theory can inform practice and we suggested that practices are often based upon some theory. The principles identified above can be located within theoretical traditions and frameworks. Theory can help us find a reasoned and systematic approach to individual moral problems and can inform the kind of practical judgement that we need in order to make decisions. We now examine, briefly, some of the main theoretical traditions.

Deontological theories

These theories maintain that the right action to pursue is independent of the consequences of that action. The right action, from this perspective, would be to keep a promise, repay a debt or abide by a contract irrespective of what the consequences are. There are many non-consequentialist relationships such as friendship, or parent-child relationships where special obligations arise by virtue of that relationship. What is important is the quality of the relationship rather than the ends for which it is intended. The most famous philosopher associated with this approach to ethics is Immanuel Kant (1724–1804). Kant believed that an act is morally praiseworthy only if done neither for self-interested reasons nor as a result of natural disposition but rather from *duty*; not just in accordance with duty but for the sake of duty. It is not praiseworthy to perform a morally right action, because this could stem from self-interest. Often duty and self-interest do coincide but, for Kant, a moral action is performed out of duty even though it may be against self-interest. Kant argued that persons must never be treated as the means to an end, but as having their own autonomously established goals.

'I ought never to act in such a way except that I can also will that my maxim should become a universal law.' This is the famous categorical imperative. It is categorical because it admits no exceptions and is absolutely binding. It is imperative because it gives instructions on how to act: 'help others in distress', 'treat people equally' or 'pay people fairly'. Individuals and organizations cannot make an exception for themselves.

People can be treated as ends in order, for example, to achieve organizational goals, but they should be treated with respect and dignity at all times so that they do not become merely servants or objects and are not used exclusively for another's ends. This approach is about treating other people as we would like to be treated ourselves – with respect, dignity and courtesy – as much in our organizational lives as our social lives. Some actions are wrong for reasons other than their consequences. For Kant, the features of an action that make it right are not dependent upon any particular outcome. There are many special relationships that depend upon commitment, trust and duty and these are non-consequentialist. Professional relationships are often seen in these terms. The doctor has a duty of care towards the patient, the teacher towards the student. Indeed, the public official generally is characterized as having a public service ethos, a duty to act on behalf of the public. Quinlan (1993) recognizes the importance of role for the public services manager. His concern is with the duties of senior officials and he argues that accompanying that role are duties of care about facts and proper process, duties of balance in argument, and duties of frankness in advice.

Of course, such duties and imperatives are, in practice, overridden. They can come into conflict with each other; we do break promises if we believe that to do so will do more good than harm or to prevent suffering. If we consider, for example, truth-telling in healthcare provision, it can be seen in a number of different ways:

- Tell the truth, since patients and their loved ones are better off when informed of their diagnoses and prognoses and can make plans to best provide for their families.
- Tell the truth, since patients have a right to know.
- Telling the truth can be painful for the patient and cause them harm.
- Patients with serious conditions may not want to know and withholding information may not be a violation of their rights.

What we have are arguments both for and against the universal principle that the truth should always be told.

However, arguments from a deontological perspective place responsibility on the individual. The notion that public officials are there to carry out the policies of their political masters is undermined by the view that obedience to ethical principles is of fundamental importance. As it becomes increasingly recognized that public services managers at all levels have scope for discretion and that 'freedom to manage' becomes a management imperative, adherence to a set of ethical principles will guide the managers' behaviour.

Teleological theories

These theories provide the second major guide to moral decisions where actions are evaluated in terms of their consequences. The achievement of public policy goals in terms of a better educated or a healthier citizenry would be examples of such consequences. Utilitarianism is the best known of these theories, where an action is said to be morally justifiable if it leads to the greatest happiness of the greatest number. This view is most closely associated with the work of the English philosophers Jeremy Bentham (1748–1832) and John Stuart Mill (1806–73). A version of utilitarianism is to be found in the techniques of cost benefit analysis where it is argued that it is possible to weigh up all the costs and benefits of a particular policy option through assigning numerical weighting to all the factors involved. In planning a new airport, for example, a cost benefit analysis will weigh up the costs and benefits of noise pollution, road congestion, threats to life and wildlife, threats to the quality of life, the benefits of different forms of transport and so on in as comprehensive a manner as possible. The concept of measurement is a key feature of the utilitarian approach. One immediate objection to this approach is how do you measure, for example, the quality of life? Utilitarianism is concerned with the maximization of good and the minimization of harm, howsoever defined and quantified. 'Good' may be defined, by utilitarians, as pleasure, or happiness.

Box 3.1 Utilitarianism in practice

Pete Lanner works as a surveyor for a local authority that is considering planning permission for a new out of town shopping complex. The proposed sight is on an area of grassland that is used by locals for leisure activities. There is local opposition to the plans, and among the opponents are family and friends of Mr Lanner, on the grounds that local businesses would be adversely affected and the site is used by the community for other activities. One large national retail company which intends to locate at the proposed complex has taken out an advertisement in a local newspaper advertising the positive effects that the complex will have on the local economy. The company is also aware that security of employment is not guaranteed in local government anymore, and has indicated to Mr Lanner, informally, that if the development goes ahead there may be senior positions available to manage the project. The company wishes inside information, which Mr Lanner has access to, on the way in which the planning committee is likely to vote; which councillors support the proposal and which do not. The company indicates to Mr Lanner that such an approach is not unusual and that it has adopted it successfully in other areas.

- What should Mr Lanner do?
- Which roles or interests clash?
- What general rules can be applied?

There are two different kinds of utilitarianism:

1 'Act' utilitarianism is concerned with performing that act which leads to the greatest happiness of the greatest number. Thus a rule such as 'You ought to tell the truth in making contracts' is a useful guideline but is expendable; a rule of thumb.
2 In contrast, 'rule' utilitarians hold that rules have a central place in morality that cannot be compromised by the demands of a particular situation since rules prevent us from our own shortsightedness and help us avoid acts of individual injustice in particular circumstances.

Box 3.1 gives an example of how a utilitarian approach might feature in a planning decision. Presumably, Mr Lanner will be concerned with obligations to friends and family, to the council, to his own self-interest and to the wider interests of the community. He will also be concerned with the legality and the acceptability of providing the information to the company. Mr Lanner may wish to act in such a way as to maximize benefit for the community as a whole. However, the problems with adopting a utilitarian approach are numerous:

- In practice it is not possible to review all the available options before acting.

- In promoting the greatest happiness of the greatest number, how do we weigh happiness? One possibility is through pleasure given but how do we weigh and choose between different pleasures? Is listening to Mahler's Symphony No. 5 a higher pleasure or worth more than listening to the Rolling Stones?
- We can never be sure of being able to account for all the consequences of an action.
- Over what timescale are we to calculate costs and benefits?
- Utilitarianism presupposes that we can put a quantifiable value on everything. Economists may believe this but it is fraught with difficulty. How do we measure the loss of beautiful countryside to make way for a power station that supplies us with cheaper power, or a shopping complex that provides local employment? The concern with outcomes and targets has been a particular feature of the 'new public management' that has come to characterize changes in the delivery of public services in many OECD countries. We examine the implications of this in Chapter 7.

However, before we dismiss utilitarianism completely, Pops (1994: 165) argues that:

Making moral decisions usually involves finding a balance among different values that conflict. This kind of 'moral pluralism' is highly pragmatic and well suited to the type of value diversity that characterises modern democratic societies. In terms of consequences, a realistic public administrator cannot ignore any basic moral principle that is 'out there' and likely to influence the effectiveness of the agency's mission. Tolerance thus lies at the heart of the ethical responsibility of the administrator in a democratic society. Utilitarian logic favors basing decisions on the weighted judgements of the many, and thus coincides perfectly with moral pluralism and tolerance.

The task of the public services manager is to manage among a multitude of stakeholders both internal and external to the organization and some means must be found to balance the interests of competing stakeholders.

The virtues approach

This approach was first adopted by Aristotle who thought that the possession of virtues allowed us to flourish as human beings. Aristotle's 'great, heroic leader' was characterized by courage, temperance and justice. Virtue is concerned with character, habit, and the possession of a disposition or inclination to act in a virtuous manner. It is possessed as much as exercised and is concerned with qualities of character rather than obedience to a set of ethical principles. In some ways, the virtues approach can be seen in terms of the characteristics that we believe make a good manager or a good person. What are the qualities that we admire in the manager or the individual? Confucius (the *Analects*, Book XX para. 2) identified 'five excellent practices' as virtues: 'The gentleman is generous without it costing him anything, works hard without complaining, has desires without being greedy, is casual without being arrogant, and is awe-inspiring without appearing fierce'. Both Aristotle and Confucius were concerned with what sort of life individuals ought to lead rather than what kind of actions ought to be undertaken.

More recently, MacIntyre (1981: 78) has argued for the virtues approach: 'A virtue is an acquired human quality, the possession and exercise of which tends to enable us to achieve those goods which are internal to practices and the lack of which effectively prevents us from achieving any such good'. For MacIntyre, virtue is inextricably linked to the concept of a practice which is complex but exhibits coherence, is socially established, is carried out through human cooperation, involves technical skills which are exercised within evolving traditions of values and principles and is organized to achieve certain standards of excellence. It is through the proper conduct of a practice of administration that the ends of ethical administration are achieved.

The internal goods of a practice are those that come from the satisfaction of excelling in a particular form of activity such as we may find in the concept of a professional vocation. The external goods of a practice are those that come as a result of engaging in the activity such as money, fame and power. In this sense, virtue is its own reward and results from internal goods. For MacIntyre, virtue is an acquired human quality and allows us to achieve the internal goods of a practice. Thus, if beneficence for the citizens is one of the results of public administration then benevolence on the part of managers is a virtue. If justice is an important good then fair-mindedness is a necessary attribute for administrators.

Of course it is difficult to specify just what virtues are, and they can come into conflict. Different practices may recognize different virtues. However, the importance of virtue has long been recognized in the Civil Service. The virtues associated with the Civil Service are captured in the following quote:

> They are as important today as in the last century; their importance should not diminish in the next century. We believe that the case for a permanent, politically impartial Civil Service is as compelling now as it has been for over a century. The principle of selection and promotion on merit must represent the bedrock of such a Civil Service. The importance of the values of integrity, impartiality, objectivity and accountability is rooted in the characteristics of the task which the Civil Service is called upon to perform. These values reflect rather than inhibit the jobs to be done. They are relevant to civil servants servicing the public as well as to those servicing Ministers directly.

They can and should act as a unifying force for the whole Civil Service.

(Treasury and Civil Service Committee 1994a, para 72: xvi)

Jennings (1991) argues that the virtues approach stands in contrast to regulatory ethics (i.e. that which is there to guide behaviour) because it is concerned with the agents 'being' as much as with their 'doing'. Professionals favour a virtues approach – they want their professional ethics to be characterized as virtue, character, excellence and distilled in the notion of a vocation. A virtues approach stresses individual autonomy rather than external control. Professional ethics is seen to be concerned with individual moral agency, not communal moral practice. The focus of professional ethics is on professional activity in a broad sense; activity as a form of life, a pattern of conduct revealing character, a practice of virtue and excellence. However, we might also want to focus on activity understood as decision-making and choice. Possessing virtues such as courage or wisdom is not enough – we have to see them in action. Indeed, one of the criticisms of the profession that we refer to in Chapter 5 is that in practice professionals are just as likely to act in their self-interest as anybody else and may hide behind certain myths concerning a professional ethos.

The justice approach

Justice is concerned with issues of fairness, entitlement and desert. The formal principle of justice can be seen in terms of the notion that like cases should be treated alike and unlike cases differently. Thus, equals are to be treated equally and unequals unequally. This is a controversial issue, raising issues of affirmative action and positive discrimination. For years American universities have had quota systems which allow in a certain number of students from ethnic minorities. There is currently a backlash to this with white students complaining that they have been discriminated against since they may be excluded from university despite having higher grades than a student admitted from an ethnic minority background. The argument is that universities should only admit students on merit. Justice can take two forms, distributive justice and procedural justice. The first is concerned with how goods and services are distributed within society. It is argued that the market can be unjust since it discriminates against those who are poor, uneducated and unemployed. Criteria for distributive justice, as we saw on page 37 might include:

- To each person an equal share.
- To each person according to need.
- To each person according to their individual rights.
- To each person according to individual effort.

- To each person according to individual merit.
- To each person according to contribution to society (or the organization).

Procedural justice is concerned with making sure that the processes and procedures are just and non-discriminatory. The best-known of contemporary theorists of justice is the American philosopher John Rawls (1972: 60) who argued that there are two principles of justice: 'First: each person is to have an equal right to the most extensive basic liberty compatible with similar liberty for others. Second: social and economic inequalities are to be arranged so that they are both (a) reasonably expected to be to everyone's advantage, and (b) attached to positions and offices open to all.'

Rawls asks us to conduct a thought experiment which puts us behind a 'veil of ignorance'. He argues that we would reasonably choose the two principles because any other choice may mean that we are disadvantaged since we do not know where we will be located in society and what advantages we may have in terms of being rich or poor, talented or not, male or female and so on. Thus inequalities will be tolerated if they can be expected to lead to everyone's advantage including the least advantaged.

Rights-based theories

Individuals have rights which take a number of different forms: political, legal, contractual, employee and human rights. Depending upon the society, they might include reference to the right to be treated with respect, the right to liberty compatible with the same right for everybody else, the right to a decent wage, the right to four weeks holiday with pay and so on. Some rights are positive (the right to do something) and others are negative (the right not to have liberty curtailed). Rights-based theories usually express some notion of not taking any action that infringes the agreed upon and accepted rights of others. The concept of rights tells us that employees have rights but does not tell us how rights should be balanced in practical management situations. We also need to consider duties as correlative with rights (see Box 3.2 which considers the relationship between rights and duties in the context of the relationship between employer and employee).

Principles in the public services

We take it that principles are guides to action and are built upon values. We discussed the background to the creation of the Nolan Committee to examine the ethical standards in public life in the UK in Chapter 1. The Nolan Commitee recommended a set of principles to govern public life, shown in Box 3.3.

What is the relationship between these principles and ethical theory?

Box 3.2 Employees' rights and duties

- The right to work.
- The right to just remuneration.
- The right to free association and to strike.
- The right to privacy and a normal life outside work.
- The right to fairness in contractual dealings.
- The right to participation in the decision-making processes of the organization.
- The right to a healthy and safe working environment.
- The right to job satisfaction.
- The right to be treated as individuals with status recognized and adequate training given.
- The right to be given feedback on performance at work and the opportunity to improve skills.
- The right to be paid a fair and equitable rate in relation to skills and prevailing labour market conditions.

Some of these rights may be enshrined in law (health and safety), others may have the status of aspirations (the right to adequate training). At the same time organizations may have certain duties towards their employees which are the correlative of the rights outlined above and may include the duty to inform and consult workers, to accept criticism without holding a grudge, to ensure health and safety and so on. However, the relationship cannot all be one way. In return for certain rights we might expect employees to fulfil certain duties which might include:

- The duty of loyalty.
- The duty to behave in a manner that does not harm the reputation of the organization.
- The duty to give 'a fair day's work for a fair day's pay'.
- The duty to strike only as a last resort.
- The duty to contribute to the best of their ability to the organization's goals.
- The duty to accept responsibility for developing their skills to increase their effectiveness.

---

1 Selflessness expresses a concern with the public interest, with a consequentialist approach.
2 Integrity focuses upon obligations and duties, the concern of deontological theories.
3 Objectivity involves merit and justice principles.
4 Accountability is subject to scrutiny linked to justification.
5 Openness involves the public interest.
6 Honesty is concerned with duties and conflicts of interest.
7 Leadership extols the virtues.

In practice, the Nolan principles are based upon a range of ethical theories. This is always the case. However, managers themselves may not necessarily agree with the principles laid down by Nolan. The seven features

---

Box 3.3 The seven principles of public life

1 **Selflessness:** holders of public office should take decisions solely in terms of the public interest. They should not do so in order to gain financial or other material benefits for themselves, their family or their friends.
2 **Integrity:** holders of public office should not place themselves under any financial or other obligations to outside individuals or organizations that might influence them in the performance of their official duties.
3 **Objectivity:** in carrying out public business, including making public appointments, awarding contracts or recommending individuals for rewards and benefits, holders of public office should make choices on merit.
4 **Accountability:** holders of public office are accountable for their decisions and actions to the public and must submit themselves to whatever scrutiny is appropriate to their office.
5 **Openness:** holders of public office should be as open as possible about all the decisions and actions that they take. They should give reasons for their decisions and restrict information only when the wider public interest clearly demands it.
6 **Honesty:** holders of public office have a duty to declare any private interest relating to their public duties and to take steps to resolve any conflicts arising in a way that protects the public interest.
7 **Leadership:** holders of public office should promote and support these principles by leadership and example.

Source: Nolan Committee 1995 (Crown copyright is reproduced with the permission of the Controller of Her Majesty's Stationery Office)

---

of Nolan were included in a questionnaire as part of a range of questions designed to elicit information concerning the principles and qualities of public services management. The OUBS research referred to in the previous chapter revealed the results shown in Table 3.1.

Comparing the response to the questionnaire with the Nolan principles we find that:

1 Selflessness featured in 10th and 17th positions.
2 Integrity is in 1st and 8th positions.
3 Objectivity is in 6th and 15th positions.
4 Accountability is in 2nd and 6th positions.
5 Openness is in 4th and joint 10th positions.
6 Honesty is in 8th and joint 10th positions.
7 Leadership is in 9th and 14th positions.

This is hardly a ringing endorsement for Nolan! However, the difficulty of developing a set of principles for public services managers is recognized by theorists. Wanna *et al.* (1992: 209) argue that ethical standards are difficult to classify and define, and that ethical frameworks have developed as a result of government policy, legislative requirements and financial and administrative codes, guidelines and conventions:

Table 3.1 OUBS research: respondents were asked to rank up to 12 in order of importance

What do you think **should** be the key principles for managing the public services?		What do you think **are** the key principles for managing the public services?	
Position	Respondents who gave it a ranking(%)	Position	Respondents who gave it a ranking(%)
1 Integrity	100	1 Meeting targets	85
2 Accountability	100	2 Obeying rules	70
3 Responding to the client/customer	85	Obeying superiors	55
4 Openness	85	4 Political awareness	90
5 Committed to public service ethos	80	5 Competitiveness	52
6 Objectivity	77	6 Accountability	95
7 Loyalty	50	7 Responding to the client/customer	70
8 Honesty	88	8 Integrity	68
9 Leadership	73	9 Opportunism	72
10 Selflessness	20	10 Honesty	40
11 Meeting targets	55	Openness	28
12 Thoroughness	62	12 Working hard	62
13 Exercising initiative	72	Committed to public service ethos	47
14 Working hard	50	14 Leadership	65
15 Opportunism	17	15 Objectivity	55
Competitiveness	17	16 Loyalty	40
17 Loyalty	50	17 Thoroughness	35
18 Obeying rules	25	Selflessness	33
19 Obeying superiors	0	19 Exercising initiative	22

Ethical standards in the public sector emanate from the practical operation of a political system of administration. Ethics are not god-given, invariable creeds which are imposed on the system from without. Rather ethical behaviour is a constantly refreshed conventional code of practice which largely originates from within. In this sense, political conventions, value expectations, bureaucratic norms, legislative requirements and formal and informal codes of conduct all combine to produce a somewhat ambiguous mix of ethical practices.

This viewpoint is consistent with that expressed earlier by MacIntyre (1981) who locates virtues within the context of a practice. Denhardt (1991: 97)

argues that virtue should be reinvigorated as the basis for ethics in the public services and defines the moral foundations of public administration as consisting of honour, benevolence, and justice: 'Putting too much faith in institutional arrangements and processses for the resolution to problems of bad decisions, unethical conduct, or abuse of administrative authority encourages us to lose sight of the real purposes of those institutions and instead to focus only on perfecting rules, regulations, and control mechanisms that will yield more ethical outcomes'.

The findings of the Public Accounts Committee discussed in Chapter 2 (see pages 23–4) would support the notion that the last thing we need is more systems of control at an institutional level. Controls can take place at different levels: individual, peer group, institutional and societal. Problems can arise when they serve different values and purposes: e.g. institutional arrangements may serve accountability, instrumental values may serve efficiency and fundamental values serve honesty and fairness. Not only that but principles are often mixed up with the virtues necessary to carry out those principles. Virtues are necessary to bring ethical principles into moral practice. We can represent this as follows:

VALUE → PRINCIPLE → VIRTUE → PRACTICE

Thus injunctions to always act for the greater good requires a virtue such as courage to put them into practice, particularly when others may be harmed. According to Denhardt (1991), honour is the adherence to the highest standards of responsibility, integrity and principle. It is a quality of character, the pre-eminent virtue, and the basis for public confidence. Benevolence is the 'other-regarding' character of public service and it requires not just doing good but also a driving motivation to do good for the sake of others. It is linked to the public service ethos and can be used to judge when a conflict of interest arises as a result of institutional obligations on the part of public officials. Justice is concerned with fairness and regard for the rights of others. Denhardt argues that we need a combination of core values.

In a similar fashion, Gillon (1994: 184) argues that: '. . . whatever our personal philosophy, politics, religion, moral theory, or life stance, we will find no difficulty in committing ourselves to four prima facie moral principles plus a reflective concern about their scope of application'. These principles are, first, respect for autonomy, which in the context of healthcare means respecting the rights of patients and respecting confidentiality. This could be seen from a Kantian perspective. Second and third, beneficence and non-maleficence are taken together and stipulate that we must help people without harming others. This means, for example, providing net benefits to patients and being clear about the risks involved based upon all available information. This might be seen from a utilitarian perspective. Fourth, justice, which is concerned with fair distribution of scarce resources (distributive justice), respect for people's rights (rights-based justice) and respect for morally acceptable laws (legal justice).

In some ways the support for a set of core principles might be compared to the core competencies that are so familiar to readers of management textbooks. Management textbooks are usually full of prescriptions advocating the qualities that managers (usually senior) should possess. Schroeder (1989), for example, lists eleven high perfomance managerial qualities and senior managers are required to perform four different roles which exhibit these qualities:

1 A strategic role which identifies the direction in which the organization should be moving. An achievement orientation towards task completion along with the qualities of a visionary would be required.
2 A coordinating role to make sure that everybody is moving in the same direction. Power-broking skills would be required here.
3 A troubleshooting role to sort out any problems. Negotiating skills will be important here.
4 A leadership role which will also require the skills of communication and presentation to those within and outside the organization, where the role of a figurehead will feature.

To accompany these, managers are expected to be highly motivated, to work on their own and yet to be good 'team players', to possess technical expertise and to be achievers. In comparison, Aristotle's heroic leader probably had it easy! An example of the demands placed upon public services managers is illustrated in Box 3.4.

Box 3.4 Australian public service values

A set of general principles are prescribed which guide the activities of the Australian public official:

1 The highest standards of probity, integrity and conduct demonstrated by:
 ● acting in accordance with the letter and spirit of the law;
 ● dealing equitably, honestly and responsively with the public;
 ● avoiding real or apparent conflicts of interest.

2 A strong commitment to the community shown by:
 ● protecting members of the community from arbitrary or discriminatory treatment by public service staff;
 ● protecting the privacy of members of the community;
 ● implementing legislation and government policy without imposing unnecessary burdens on the community.

3 Responsiveness to governments shown by:
 ● serving loyally and impartially ministers and the government;
 ● providing frank, honest and comprehensive advice;
 ● actively facilitating the implementation of government policies.

4 A strong commitment to accountability demonstrated by:
  - contributing fully to the accountability of the agency to the government, of the government to the parliament and of the parliament to the people;
  - fully supporting the administrative and legal measures established to enhance accountability;
  - recognizing that those delegating authority for performance do not lose responsibility and may be called to account.

5 A close focus on results shown by:
  - pursuing efficiency and effectiveness at all levels;
  - delivering services to the public conscientiously and courteously;
  - making decisions and taking actions in a timely and competent manner.

6 Continuous improvement by teams and individuals through:
  - striving for creativity and innovation;
  - making individual and team performance count.

7 Merit as the basis for achieving excellence in staffing by:
  - ensuring equality of opportunity;
  - providing fair and reasonable rewards as an incentive to high performance.

Source: Management Advisory Board 1996

Conclusion

Both theorists and practitioners implicitly are saying that a range of principles should be taken together rather than just relying on one, that these principles are derived from some more fundamental theory, and expressing them as principles seems to capture their operational imperative. Public services managers are as much concerned with how services are delivered as what is delivered. In the example shown in Box 3.4 Australian public officials are enjoined to 'deliver services to the public conscientiously and courteously'. Looking after clients' interests means treating them with care, attention and sensitivity; indeed, as Kant would enjoin us, treating them with respect.

four

The public service ethos

Key issues

- The meaning of the public service ethos for different groups of managers.
- The nature and location of the public service ethos.
- The alleged decline of the public service ethos.

Introduction

It is part of conventional wisdom that those working in the public services are bound by, and in most cases subscribe to, a public service ethos. That this ethos is, in some way, considered to be a 'good thing' is taken for granted by practitioners and commentators alike. The ethos is traditionally characterized as comprising honesty, integrity, impartiality, recruitment and promotion on merit, probity, accountability and, indeed, many of the virtues discussed in Chapter 3. In the UK it has its roots in the Northcote-Trevelyan Report (1854) on the Civil Service and the key features of this ethos can be found in the workings of the public services elsewhere. The Treasury and Civil Service Committee report (1994a) on the UK Civil Service reaffirmed the central tenets of the ethos. This report also argued that such characteristics form a unified UK Civil Service. In Australia the Commonwealth government's Management Advisory Board in its report *Building A Better Public Service* (1993) similarly reinforced the principles of impartiality, probity, integrity and accountability.

The public service ethos is associated with a notion of acting in the public interest. The public interest, as a concept, has played a key role in theorizing about the relations between government and its citizens throughout history. It has, at various times, been described as the 'common good' or the 'general will' and its promotion has been seen as the appropriate role for goverment and is premised on the existence of a common life. However, its definition has not been straightforward. Who, or what, is to constitute the public? Is an interest to be defined in terms of a hobby or a material stake in an institution or state of affairs, and is the public interest merely the sum of private interests? Thucydides in his *History of the Peloponnesian War* expressed the view that: 'Leaders of parties in cities had programmes which appeared admirable . . . but in professing to serve the public interest they were seeking to win prizes for themselves' (Book III p. 210).

There is undoubtedly a commendatory value to notions of the public interest such that if an action can be justified in terms of the public interest then it is in some sense deemed to be a good thing. This can be linked to our discussion of utilitarianism and the difficulties identified in determining who benefits and how it can be measured. Thus, the injunction 'always act in the public interest' is not always clear-cut. Indeed, within government, sectional interests often prevail. Watt (1988) describes how departmental interests dominate Westminster such that there is no dominant voice in Cabinet actually arguing for the public interest. Cosy links between departments and their constituents and clients can also exist. In Chapter 2 we referred to the 'revolving door' syndrome. As we shall also see, fragmentation of government to semi-autonomous units may mean that a strategic perspective, part of which should include the public interest, is lacking.

An assessment of the public interest cannot be divorced from a consideration of who will be accountable for it. In a democracy its promotion is deemed to be in the hands of the politician rather than the manager. There are limits to how far an appointed official can be seen to be determining the public interest. Indeed one of the criticisms made of the senior Civil Service by Margaret Thatcher was that it manipulated politicians to further its own interest. We discuss the relationship between civil servants and their ministers in Chapter 5. The role of the public services manager will be complicated by the tensions between the values of democracy and the bureaucratic concerns with efficiency and economy.

Pugh (1991) identifies a bureaucratic ethos which comprises efficiency, expertise, efficacy, loyalty and accountability and is concerned with process rather than outcome. The public service ethos then may be located in either a bureaucratic ethos or a democratic ethos or both. According to Pugh the democratic ethos consists of regime values, citizenship, public interest and social equity. Can bureaucracy enhance these values? Is democracy concerned with ends and bureaucracy with means? Where do notions of the good life or the common good fit in? A bureaucratic ethos may be linked to instrumental rationality. Pugh argues that the two are not complementary to each other and may be alternatives or even threats to each other. We examine the impact of bureaucracy on public services managers in Chapter 6.

We also need to consider the status of an ethos. It is generally considered to be something we live, a way of life which may be ethical. We could have a professional ethos, a bureaucratic ethos and a democratic ethos all in tension. Crucial characteristics about a way of life are that we learn it, it is transmitted over time, and it has its own language. Recall the concept of a practice, associated with the work of MacIntyre, that was discussed in the previous chapter.

As far as the public service ethos is concerned the strength of this ethos is indicated when standards of conduct in public life are perceived not to measure up and public outcry results. In the UK the Nolan Committeee was set up as just such a response to a perceived decline in the standards of public life (see Chapter 3). In the UK, and elsewhere, the standards of conduct of public services managers have been under threat as a result of changes in accountability, roles, structures and public expectations and the adoption of techniques, ideas and personnel from the private sector. The common public service ethos is assumed to be in decline.

William Plowden, a former senior UK civil servant, has argued that the relationship between ministers and senior officials is under threat because of changes in accountability, roles and expectations. Similar fears were expressed by Robert Sheldon MP in evidence given to the Treasury and Civil Service Committee (1994). Why such concerns and why now? Much is due to the impact of the management reforms that have been introduced in many OECD countries since the early 1980s. However, the assumption of a common ethos begs the questions of who defines it, who owns it, how is it transmitted, what affects its continuity over time, can it be evaluated, and is it universal? The characterization of the public service ethos as commonly understood may be appropriate for certain groups of managers performing certain tasks but not for all. *The Next Steps* report (Efficiency Unit 1988), which laid the foundations for the creation of agencies in the UK, was quite clear that the concept of a career in a unified Civil Service may be redundant if the fragmentation into agencies takes place. However, a discussion of the public service ethos will now be conducted by investigating a series of propositions.

Proposition 1: there exists a public service ethos

That there exists a public service ethos is often taken for granted by politicians, officials and commentators alike. Sir Robin Butler, the head of the UK Civil Service, has argued that the Civil Service is 'unified but not uniform' (Treasury and Civil Service Committee 1989: 348). Denis Ives, the public services commissioner for the Australian Commonwealth government has argued that:

> The traditional concept of a career service would encompass the notion that public service is a vocation for life; its functions and responsibilities are essentially different from those of other occupations and requires different skills; it has a hierarchical structure of positions; it has a uniform framework of regulations, pay, conditions and work practices; and it has a shared set of values and principles focusing on merit and integrity.
>
> (Ives 1994: 7)

The ethos concerns a set of values held in common by officials expressed through the possession of a number of virtues which are exercised in the delivery of public services. These virtues are commonly understood as having weight and count towards inclusion as 'one of us'. The English obsession with cricket ensures that the official who possesses these virtues has 'a safe pair of hands' or 'can bat on a sticky wicket'.

Pratchett and Wingfield (1994) in their research on the public service ethos in UK local government describe a generic public service ethos comprising accountability, bureaucratic behaviour, a sense of community, motivation and loyalty. However, two main assumptions are made concerning the ethos. First, that there is something distinctive about managing in the public services. Second, that there is a common ethos that binds those who work in the public services together. Those who endorse the first assumption argue that there are differences between the public and the private sectors which include: the statutory framework within which most public services operate; the public sector's concern with equitable outcomes; the processes and structures adopted to achieve a complexity of goals; the recipient of services being the citizen generally or the client rather than the customer; and that public services are uniform services provided nationally. Thus, Stewart and Ranson (1988) argue, as we discussed in Chapter 1, that the purposes, the conditions and the tasks of public service are distinctive. However, the assertions concerning the distinctiveness of the public sector have not gone unchallenged. It has been argued that the difference between the two sectors is increasingly blurred, that the private sector also operates within a legal framework, that private sector organizations do operate corporate social responsibility and that the tasks of the two sectors are often similar (see Murray 1975).

The second assumption is that the ethos is unified. However, the characteristics of the public service ethos as outlined above may be appropriate for certain groups of officials performing certain tasks but can it be applied universally? Indeed, as Downs (1967) argued, individual officials may be motivated by a mixture of self-interest and altruism.

It can be argued that the concept of a unified and uniform Civil Service, let alone the public services in general, has little meaning for most civil servants. The Civil Service performs a number of different tasks which include the analysis of policy issues, the formation of policy under political direction, the implementation of policy, the delivery of services to the public, the management of resources, the regulation of outside bodies and so on. In the UK Civil Service, policy work is only carried out by some 10 per cent of the Civil Service and yet the concerns of those civil servants engaged in such work has, to all intent and purposes, dominated the agenda. In the UK the Whitehall 'village' with its own language, conventions, rules of the game and ways of working remains powerful. This 'way of life' was challenged during the 1980s and relations between the senior Civil Service and ministers came under strain during the era of commitment politics. In an age of conviction politics the concept of neutral and impartial advice comes under threat: '... if civil servants fear that their cherished neutrality is being eroded and therefore continue, possibly with some justification, to hawk their consciences around, maybe Ministers will, in turn, be tempted to rely increasingly on political sympathisers whom they feel they can trust' (Plowden 1985: 395).

The concept of trust is a key factor in the informal relations that tend to operate in government whether it be between politicians and officials or among officials themselves and we examine it in more detail in Chapter 5. In their study of Whitehall, Heclo and Wildavsky point to the importance of trust between officials in the village community that is said to characterize Whitehall. Such trust is a product of shared standards and understandings which have been developed over time, forming part of a tradition and which may not be shared by the politician (see Heclo and Wildavsky 1981). One of the architects of the modern UK Civil Service, Sir Warren Fisher (1928: 22), indicated that: 'Practical rules ... depend ... as much on the instinct and perceptions of the individuals as upon cast-iron formulas; and the surest guide will always be found in the nice and jealous honour of the civil servants themselves'.

There is a fear that trust broke down when the position of the senior Civil Service was seen to be undermined during the Thatcher years. Criticizing the notion of the detached official, John Hoskyns, a policy advisor to Margaret Thatcher, argued that the sense of detachment, one of the virtues that senior officials had prided themselves on, also created a sense of distance as though officials were engaged in policy advice to a 'far-away country which they serve only on a retainer basis' (see Young 1990: 339).

Throughout the 1980s in the UK relations between the Civil Service and politicians were deteriorating. Critics of the Civil Service argued that the game was up and that reform was needed. No longer could the civil servant be allowed the power so amusingly depicted in the *Yes Minister* television programmes. Critics argued that the traditional public service ethos was dysfunctional for government in that:

- The agenda for the Civil Service had been controlled by those at the top.
- This agenda reflected the interests of the small number of policy advisers.
- This has been perpetrated over time through recruitment by the senior Civil Service 'in its own image'.
- This was reinforced through training 'on the job' which limited exposure to outside influences and by tried and tested promotion routes through the Treasury or through the prime minister's office.

Similar cries for reform were heard elsewhere and in Australia, for example, change was perceived to be less threatening not least because the policy style of Premier Hawke was less combative than that of Margaret Thatcher in the UK. Hawke came into power with a detailed plan for reforming the Civil Service and his proposals fell on fertile ground. According to Zifcak (1994) the mandarin elite was being replaced by a younger breed of 'managerial technocrats', committed to reform. At the same time, the isolated position of Canberra encouraged close relationships between senior officials, and the smaller size of government in Canberra encouraged a commonality of view.

In local government and in health services in the UK the agenda was dominated by a different set of stakeholders, notably professionals. Pratchett and Wingfield (1994: 14) question the assumption of a generic public service ethos in local government: '. . . the public service ethos is a confused and ambiguous concept which is only given meaning by its organisational and functional situation, and may be subject to very different interpretations over both time and location'. They argue that there are differences within and between local authorities because of two key factors. First, the role of local government is interpreted differently, partly depending upon the political make-up of the particular authority. As a result, one role played by local authorities is that of the minimalist authority which encourages other organizations to provide services, determined by the market. In the authority that most closely resembled this model, Pratchett and Wingfield found that managers much more readily questioned the existence of the public service ethos than their counterparts in other local authorities who saw themselves more readily engaging with the wider community in partnership to develop that community. Different authorities will adopt a different ethos varying between a community-based approach and a commercial approach. The second key factor, according to Pratchett and Wingfield, is the diversity of professional backgrounds of those who work in local government which makes it difficult to develop a common ethos nationally. Professionals may look to their own profession rather than to the particular organization within which they find themselves. Professions are said to possess a number of defining characteristics which include the application of skills based upon technical knowledge; this knowledge being acquired through advanced training and education. Entry to the profession is through some formal testing of competence and there are controls on admission to the profession usually administered by the profession itself. There is in existence a professional association and this association will have codes of conduct to regulate the activities of its members and to set standards. For those working within the public services, there is considered to be a commitment or calling or sense of responsibility for, and to, the public.

The professions are many and varied and include those working in central government such as statisticians, accountants or engineers who are said to be 'on tap rather than on top'; in health services they will include members of the medical profession; in local government they will also include town planners, solicitors, teachers, and, arguably, social workers. To draw a boundary around these groups is rather arbitrary, particularly, as discussed in the next section, since management reforms have had an impact upon professional practices. However, a major issue in the role of professionals is, as Benveniste (1987) has suggested, the substitution of routine roles by discretionary ones. Discretion is required where, according to Benveniste, we do not know what the problem is, or where we know what is to be achieved but are not sure how, or when we know what the goals are and how to achieve them but the tasks are so varied and changing that constant adaptation is needed. As discretion widens so does the scope for different practices being adopted.

A further consideration is the importance of differential information where the professional acts on behalf of his or her client (see Wrigley and McKevitt 1994). For example, in healthcare the doctor is not merely a provider of medicine but also an agent of the client in providing information – a dual role. Allocation of resources is measured by professional standards and judgement, and trust is crucial. There is often high risk for the client. Increasingly, with pressures on resources, professionals may be holding the line between the desires for cost containment and the threat of a decline in service quality. Proximity to the client is a feature of the work of those professionals engaged in front-line service delivery and this can cause tensions. Bertilsson (1990) illustrates the dual role of the professional servicing the individual client and the citizenry as a whole. In the range of commitments that a professional engages in, the commitment to some notion of the public good may be low down on the list of priorities. Traditionally, professionals, in particular those associated with the caring services, are engaged in one-to-one relationships with clients within a reciprocal relationship of duties and obligations. A further set of relationships involves fellow professionals, and professional codes of conduct may regulate those relationships. Furthermore, the notion of the public service ethos being defined by professionals needs to recognize that there are different groups of professionals with different interests. The status of different professionals is changing and will continue to change as the conditions of their engagement with government change.

The existence of a public service ethos is not proven. Indeed it is unlikely that, given the variety of roles, tasks and values that characterize diverse public services, it could ever exist.

Proposition 2: the public service ethos is under threat from management reforms that have taken place in recent years

The driving forces for change are well documented and, to recall the discussion in Chapter 1, include the pressure on public expenditure as a result of economic recession, public disenchantment with the quality of public services, the influence of New Right philosophy and the belief in markets as the best economic model for resource allocation. As a result many OECD countries adopted a reform programme with similar features. These included a greater focus on performance, a focus on outcomes rather than processes, increased value for money, enhanced flexibility to respond to what became known as the customer, strengthened accountability, control and efficiency. In Australia the reform framework included: more ministerial control over departments; more positive response from officials; providing officials with greater flexibility and authority; a focus on outcomes and accountability for results; a stress on the strategic view; a focus on meeting client needs; and a demand for high standards of probity and integrity while at the same time satisfying staff (see Management Advisory Board 1993).

In the UK the financial management initiative and the introduction of Next Steps Agencies were designed to make managers more accountable, to push responsibility downwards, to respond to what was now known as the customer. In the NHS and local government, purchaser-provider splits were created and quasi-markets introduced. The private sector was encouraged to provide services previously thought to be within the domain of the public sector.

The content of reforms was similar in both Australia and the UK but the reform process was markedly different. According to Zifcak (1994), in Australia both politicians and officials were interested in reform. As already indicated, in the UK Margaret Thatcher's style was perceived to be conflictual in contrast to the collaborative style and broker role adopted by Premier Bob Hawke in Australia (see Campbell and Halligan 1992). There appeared to be less antagonism to change in Australia. There was an environment conducive to change supported by senior politicians and officials. According to Zifcak, reform works best where there is strong political interest in, and commitment to, it; it will proceed more effectively where there is a commonality of view between ministers and civil servants; it will be successful where a government remains in power for a long period of time; and it will be better received if it has strong parliamentary support. In contrast to the senior Civil Service in the UK, the senior Civil Service in Australia had a background that made them more receptive to change and more willing to accept reform. This background has been termed 'economic rationalist' (see Pusey 1991).

The existence of the public sector ethos has been questioned not least because of fears that the new world of public sector management has undermined many of the traditional virtues associated with public administration. The belief in managers (which appears to have replaced the belief that professionals play the key role in delivering public services) means that:

- The role of managers has been greatly enhanced and there is a belief that greater managerial responsibility and autonomy will increase organizational effectiveness.
- This has necessitated the development of new managerial skills.
- The exercise of these skills will be subject to performance evaluation and review.

The success of public services organizations is increasingly premised upon the skill of managers in fostering 'proactive mindsets': in becoming more entrepreneurial and innovative, performing to meet targets and so on. According to one chief executive of an Australian government business enterprise, 'My biggest problem is changing the mindset of staff from a professional culture to a performance culture' (personal interview, September 1994). The development of competencies is seen as the key to management success, and hence organizational success. In moving from professionalism to managerialism we have seen a move from duty to performance.

The civil servant is said to possess probity, impartiality, intellectual rigour, frankness, independence of mind, adaptability, energy, political awareness, good oral and written communication skills, negotiating ability and a thorough knowledge of government and parliamentary processes. These skills are welcomed by ministers. However, public officials are expected to acquire new skills which include a team-building approach, a willingness to be innovative, firmness when confronting poor performance, imagination and flair, listening skills and contract management skills (see Cabinet Office 1993: 27). However, when public services managers are encouraged to be more like their private sector counterparts they may well encounter difficulties in learning new techniques and indeed a new language. New skills might include the need to write or judge a business plan, how to specify and monitor contracts, or how to price outputs in a competitive environment. The new language will include the concepts of markets, prices, contracts, competitors, customers, business units, profit centres and so on (see Mackintosh 1995).

What has been the impact of these changes on the public service ethos? We can examine a number of key areas.

The first is structural reform. Many of the changes involved structural reform and the fragmentation of service delivery into business units or into arms-length agencies along the lines of Next Steps in the UK or Government Business Enterprises (GBE) in Australia. The rationale for structural change is to push responsibility downwards, to create flatter organizations, to separate policy formulation and implementation, or to 'get closer to the customer'. A consequence of this, according to some critics, is that the fragmentation of service delivery erodes the collegial sense of belonging to a community of like-minded individuals pursuing a common goal. As one senior manager in a GBE put it, 'Cost centres are like alley cats and will cut another cost centre's throat' (personal interview, September 1994). However, departmentalism has always operated where departmental cultures are different and where there is competition for scarce resources. Not only that, but cosy relationships have, in some cases, existed between departments and their clients and some departments have been 'captured' by outside bodies.

The second area is control. In order for the structural reforms to work then control has to be given up by those at the centre to managers working at the front line. If delegated responsibility is to make sense then managers have to be trusted. In the UK it has proven difficult to remove the hand of the Treasury and allow managers 'freedom to manage'.

The third area concerns processes. The acceptance of bureaucratic rules has diminished as managers are encouraged to be more entrepreneurial. The reforms stress outcomes rather than process. As one Canberra official put it, 'The focus on outcomes is good whereas the obsession with process is unhealthy. Process became the end of public service' (personal interview, September 1994). However, as public services are increasingly delivered through a wider range of organizations, including those from the private sector, there is a danger of throwing the process baby out with the bathwater. As new relationships are formed something has to be put in place to regulate these relationships. In the past, traditional ways of working and the existence of informal conventions acted as a framework for officials' behaviour. There is a danger that if these relationships are undermined, or are no longer perceived to be relevant, then a vacuum may occur.

A good example of this was illustrated in the UK Committee of Public Accounts report (1994), discussed in Chapter 2. Investigating alleged corruption, the committee found that every case examined involved breaches of existing rules or guidelines and argued that more detailed rules were not required. Failures resulted from inadequate financial controls, failure to comply with rules, inadequate stewardship of public money and assets, and failure to provide value for money. The reasons advanced for this included inexperienced staff, poor monitoring, failure to pursue money owed, failure to establish clear lines of accountability, failure to take prompt action, failure to make regular reviews, and possible conflicts of interest.

Rather than finding evidence of corrupt officials the committee found the breakdown of existing processes. As public sector officials deal more and more with the private sector it is a moot point whether they have skills in contract management. It is a new experience for many managers. The first Nolan Report recognized that increased responsibility for front-line managers may confront them with ethical issues with which they had had no previous experience (Nolan Committee 1995: para. 61). Interestingly enough in the first two years in the life of the ICAC in New South Wales 7 of the 19 key issues examined were concerned with dealings between the public and private sectors.

The fourth area is the impact upon professionals. One of the results of the 'new managerialism' has been to undermine the power and autonomy of professionals. Gyford (1993) contrasts professionalism with managerialism and argues that:

- Professionals perceive the public as clients rather than customers.
- The basis of evaluation is professional standards rather than performance indicators.
- A professional ethos is based on mystery rather than on clarity.
- The mode of evaluation is based on judgement and not measurement.

Critics argue that the public service ethos should derive from the democratic system rather than from professional practice.

The fifth area concerns people; the use of managers from outside the service has been encouraged in an attempt to create a more enterprising and entrepreneurial culture. In giving evidence to the Nolan Committee (1995, paras 1074 and 1080) both Sir John Bourn (the comptroller and auditor general) and Robert Sheldon MP expressed concern at the effect on the public service ethos of the involvement of senior staff brought in from outside, unaccustomed to standards and not imbued with the ethos. There are fears that cost efficiency would replace traditional values and the 'ethics of a dollar saved' would become paramount. One union representative of public officials in Canberra expressed the view that bringing in outsiders created problems: 'They are prepared to turn a blind eye to certain practices. They look to the interests of their firms rather than the taxpayer' (personal interview, September 1994). A similar view was expressed by a union official representing local government officers in the UK where professional work is being put out to competitive tendering: 'It may be that the loyalties of such professionals will switch from the local authority representing the community to the interests of the particular firm' (personal interview, January 1995).

In New South Wales the appointment of chief executives from outside government has not met with great success for two main reasons. First, such outsiders have difficulty in coming to terms with the rules of the game and the bureaucratic practices and second, they have difficulty in coping with the political environment and working through politicians. As one New South Wales cabinet official put it: 'There was originally a naive belief in "fresh blood" from outside' (personal interview, September 1994).

The use of managers from outside the Civil Service has been used in an attempt to create a more enterprising and entrepreneurial culture. In giving evidence to the Nolan Committee, Sir Michael Quinlan, former permanent secretary at the Ministry of Defence argued that: '. . . people who have come in from outside . . . bring many strengths but who have not absorbed the ethos with their mother's milk' (Quinlan 1995: 239). At the same time, the skills of the senior Civil Service are precisely in knowing the machinery of government. They possess the ability to draft elegant responses to parliamentary questions and be attuned to political sensitivities. However, in the UK there is little evidence of the public sector being 'corrupted' by individuals brought in from outside; 35 out of the first 98 chief executives of Next Steps Agencies were appointed from outside the Civil Service (often from other parts of the public sector) yet these 35 make up less than 0.2 per cent of the top seven grades and many of these are in charge of the agencies with less than 2000 staff and are below the senior open structure 1–3. Indeed the Oughton Report (Cabinet Office 1993) argued for greater exposure to outside organizations.

The sixth area is accountability. The creation of different types of agencies has led to concerns about the fragmentation of accountability. In the UK there has been concern about the growth in unelected bodies to deliver public services, concern with the relationship between chief executives and ministers and concern with devolving too much responsibility to front-line managers in decentralized units. It is now recognized that there are different forms of accountability operating at different levels. However, the issue remains contentious. One senior manager in an Australian government business enterprise argued that: 'Accountability requirements are a disadvantage, particularly as we are not spending taxpayers money' (personal interview, September 1994). Dunleavy and Hood (1994) argue that the public management debate has not yet succeeded in delineating what should be the essential tasks of government. This being the case, it is likely that accountability for what and to whom will continue to be contested.

The seventh area is business techniques. A feature of the reform in both Australia and the UK has been the adoption of business practices. A key difference, however, is that the Australian approach appears to have been more pragmatic and has created business enterprises where appropriate rather than the wholesale adoption of a market philosophy. As New South Wales officials argue: 'It is whether an organization is a monopoly rather than whether it is in the public or private sector that is the key' (personal interview, September 1994).

The eighth and final area is performance and pay, whereby the concept of a unified service is deemed to be under threat from local pay bargaining and from the introduction of performance-related pay. Local pay bargaining will increase differentials and the introduction of short-term contracts will, it is argued, undermine the concept of a career service. The UK has generally rejected, for the moment, short-term contracts for its senior Civil Service, with the exception of the chief executives of agencies, and a number of officials in Australia expressed reservations about their use. It was argued that: 'You spend the first year getting to grips with the job, the second year performing, and the third year looking for a new contract' (personal interview, September 1994).

The effects of the reforms have been mixed. According to Campbell and Halligan (1992: 34): 'Some parts of the bureaucracy have reformed themselves, others have become demoralised and still others will have remained virtually unscathed'. Given the elusiveness of the concept it is difficult to prove or disprove the claim that the public service ethos has been undermined as a result of management reforms. However, those who support the introduction of more market-like conditions for the provision of public services argue that greater competition and transparency leads to less corrupt government.

Proposition 3: the undermining of the public service ethos is a 'bad thing'

What do we mean by 'bad'? The term ethos rather than ethics has been deliberately used to be clear that they are not the same. Ethos has been used to describe a culture of work for public officials. As Dennis Ives (1994: 7) indicated, it 'is a vocation for life'. However, as previously discussed, there may be different cultures operating within the public services. Those who believe in the public service ethos identify it, in some way, with serving the public. But the public is an elusive concept. Senior civil servants serve ministers, professionals serve patients or clients, officials in agencies serve customers and so on. There are different sets of reciprocal relationships and it is here that the language of ethical behaviour is appropriate. Notions of obligations, duties, trust and rights are characteristic of such relationships. The multiple obligations of public officials has been recently recognized in the code of ethics proposed by the Association of First Division Civil Servants (FDA) which represents the interests of senior UK civil servants. The code argues that civil servants have a duty to the law both as civil servants and as citizens, that they have specific statutory duties, and that they have duties to their profession and to ministers.

According to the Australian Joint Committee of Public Accounts (1992: 12):

> The ethos of public service is the most important feature of the APS [Australian Public Service]. The Committee views with alarm the perception that, with decentralisation and devolution, the concept of working for the service is being diminished. It accepts that the emphasis on efficiency is important, but points out that a balance needs to be achieved between efficiency and aspects such as access and equity. It remains the Committee's hope that this balance can be achieved and that training . . . will restore to public servants the importance of the value of a professional public administration.

If the public service ethos is conceived as a way of life then those whose way of life is threatened will resent it, while those whose way of life is improved may welcome the changes. Changes will affect different groups of stakeholders differently. The traditional values associated with the senior Civil Service are not values endorsed by all. John Garrett MP has argued that senior levels of the UK Civil Service suffer from management weakness and that they are remote, arrogant and inept at staff relations and personnel management. If this is the case then the mandarins are hardly likely to endear themselves to middle managers. One former senior civil servant has argued that the values of senior officials are a complex blend of, on the one hand, all the traditional virtues such as honesty, personal disinterestedness, integrity, an enormous capacity for hard work and loyalty to colleagues, but on the other hand also include traditional vices such as conservatism, caution, scepticism, elitism, a touch of arrogance and, too often, a deeply-held belief that the 'business of government can be fully understood only by government professionals' (Plowden 1994: 74).

Plowden (1994) makes the point that the Civil Service still recognizes drafting skills rather than managerial skills. Managers lower down the organization are sceptical of the abilities of those higher up. There is also a perception held by junior managers that, at the centre, much remains the same while those lower down are expected to cope with all the changes outlined in the previous section. Pratchett and Wingfield (1994) found in their research that over half the respondents to their local authority survey believed in the existence of the public service ethos and characterized it in positive terms. A further quarter defined it as a negative concept stifling initiative, bound by red tape, providing little challenge or stimulation and occasionally corrupt. A further quarter denied its existence altogether.

Of course, from the point of view of the customer, client or citizen the public sector as a whole may be criticized. As one chief executive in New South Wales expressed it: 'Too often the traditional public service ethos has meant a job for life and stuff the customer' (personal interview, September 1994).

It is difficult breaking down traditional cultures at all levels. A feature of Australian public service has been 'don't dob on your mates' and how to break down 'buddy networks'. The view that the public service ethos is beneficial is contested. It depends upon who benefits.

Conclusion

The debate among public officials, particularly in Australia, is a vigorous one concerning the dilemmas that they face as changing relationships, tasks, and values impact upon their activities. There are those who look back to a 'golden age' of public service ethos and regret its passing. In both Australia and the UK the move towards localized pay bargaining is seen to herald the end of the unified public service. This chapter has questioned whether such a service existed in the first place and has argued that the diversity of public services needs to be recognized. The 'new managerialism' may have made transparent the complexities of working within this diversity rather than brought in a new public service ethos. However, as Denis Ives (1994: 7–8) has put it, a 'new professionalism' is required which recognizes the virtues of a traditional public service ethos and includes values associated with new ways of working and new tasks. As indicated above, the public official engages in a range of relationships both inside and outside his or her organization and it may be here that a concern with ethics is located. As formal contracts replace informal arrangements and as managers develop a whole new network of relationships, then understanding those relationships may mean acquiring a new language and new ways of conceptualizing the task of the public services manager. Exposure to the market may require a more entrepreneurial, self-regulating, autonomous, proactive manager and such requirements may sit uneasily with the more traditional characteristics of the public official.

Uhr (1991) and Jennings (1991) among others have stressed the importance of virtue for public officials, expressed in terms of character, habit, disposition and so on. Traditional accounts of the public service ethos, particularly those argued for by senior officials, reflect a concern with virtues. As Macintyre (1981) has argued, virtues are exercised within a tradition or practice. One such practice may be that of the Whitehall village. The problem with such practices is that they may become obsolete, or that the outcomes of such practices may change. A common need identified by officials in Australia was to 'change the mindset' and to 'deinstitutionalize' corruption.

This chapter has examined changes in the public service ethos. It has started from the debate concerning the changing role of public services rather than from ethical debates. Arguments that in adopting private sector techniques, practices and people, the public service ethos is somehow corrupted are not convincing. Corruption has always occurred where contracts for building and land development have been given out – there is nothing new here. The pressures for immoral behaviour might come from a number of different sources depending upon existing social and bureaucratic practices which may include: obligations under traditional patterns of social life to support members of the extended family; the breakdown of traditional social controls which accompany rapid social change; the weakness of government mechanisms for enforcing rules and regulations; and the desire to circumvent what is perceived to be cumbersome government bureaucracy. The development of a public service ethos which may have general relevance becomes even more problematic if we consider the international context, notwithstanding the claims made by the OECD (1996). For example, Maheshwari (1983: 77) has argued that the social context, and the role played by public officials, is very different in some countries from that presupposed by Western liberal democracies:

> The extent of the citizens dependence on public officials in a developing country like India is not well understood in Western societies. More often than not, the citizen approaches the public servant as a supplicant without resources. The relationship is, therefore, one of dependence, not of equality. Moreover, public officials in India do not operate with the kind of legal framework that is common to many societies in the West where citizens may sue public servants for acts of either omission or commission.

The opportunity for immoral behaviour may arise because of poor leadership, low rewards and remuneration and difficulty in identifying responsibility and accountability in government. However, in commenting upon the common good, Finnis (1980: 305) argues that:

> an individual acts most appropriately for the common good, not by trying to estimate the needs of the common good 'at large', but by performing his [sic] contractual undertakings and fulfilling his other responsibilities, to other individuals . . . Fulfilling one's particular obligations . . . is necessary if one is to respect and favour the common good, *not* because 'otherwise everyone suffers', or because non-fulfillment would diminish 'overall net good' in some impossible utilitarian computation, or even because it would 'set a bad example' and thus weaken a useful practice, but simply because the common good *is* the good of individuals living together and depending upon one another in ways that favour the well-being of each.

The location of the public service ethos can be found in the working through of obligations and duties to other individuals whether colleagues, clients, customers or politicians.

five

Roles, relationships and rules

Key issues

- The different sets of relationships that exist in managing the public services.
- The content, context and limits of these relationships.
- The role of codes of conduct.
- The relationship between formal and informal rules.

Introduction

Much of the debate in recent times concerning the nature of organizational relationships has focused upon the economic model as the basis of relationships, which stresses that individuals are opportunistic, rather than the social model stressing cooperation. The economic view is limited and is predicated on the assumption that the recipient of services is a customer. One such economic model is that associated with principal-agency theory which stipulates that: contracts are crucial to relationships to protect the principal from the agent; that the protection of interests is costly to monitor; that the agent has an information advantage over the principal; and that the use of multiple performance criteria is essential. However, asymmetric information is the source of most principal-agent problems. The agent knows more than the principal, perhaps because of the technical nature of the information sought; for example, it has been argued that the civil servant can manipulate the minister because of the former's expertise in the machinery of government. Whether there is much evidence for this is

Table 5.1 Stakeholder relations

Role	Characterized by	Relations with manager	Formed by
Customer	Purchasing power	Economic exchange	Customer sovereignty
Citizen	Rights and duties	Social exchange	Equality
Client	Lack of power/ information	Professional exchange	Dependency
Minister	Authority	Hierarchical	Conventions/codes
Colleagues	Equal status	Open-ended	Friendship/loyalty
Contractors	Specifications	Contractual	Law

another matter. Former head of the Civil Service, Sir William Armstrong, argued that the Civil Service has an important role to play in formulating the framework within which ministers make their decisions (see Chapman and Greenaway 1980: 187).

However, advocates of entrepreneurial government share the same economic discourse and afford contracts a crucial role in redefining social relationships. In schools and in hospitals, for example, institutional roles are reconstituted in terms of contracts or quasi-contracts. Relationships within the public services are increasingly defined by the employer in terms of performance (instead of long-term tenure) in return for compliance and loyalty. This shift of focus is evident in accounts of accountability where constitutional authority is being supplemented (some would say replaced) by managerial accountability.

However, the responsibilities of public officials have changed and new sets of relationships, different in form and content are evident (see Table 5.1). Each of these relationships is different in kind and they will have a different ethical dimension to them, as we have already indicated. We suggested in Chapter 3 that morals are concerned with individuals acting and making decisions about a whole range of issues concerning other individuals and themselves. As individuals with consciences who choose to engage in relationships with others we will need to work out how we will treat those other individuals and how we would wish to be treated by them. It is part of the concept of the good manager that he or she is characterized as being efficient, effective, loyal to the organization, enthusiastic, committed, enterprising, resourceful etc. depending upon the kinds of values associated with managing within organizations. The qualities of the good manager may be expressed in terms of their achieving objectives and not in the conduct of their relationships despite the fact that most managers spend most of their time engaging in relationships. It is instructive to note that despite the rhetoric of managers as strategists, planners and thinkers, much of a manager's time is spent in day-to-day short-term crisis management dominated by face-to-face relationships and informal personal contacts.

Hales (1986) argues that most of the evidence seems to indicate that the notion of the manager as strategist, planner and thinker is a myth. He argues that even senior managers allow themselves to be diverted by unplanned interruptions and by informal personal contacts. Hales suggests that between two-thirds and four-fifths of a manager's time is spent in imparting or receiving information through face-to-face contact with others. In a small-scale study involving three operational managers in the UK social services, Conway (1993) found that all three managers spent:

- 23 per cent of their time exchanging information;
- 20 per cent handling papers;
- 22 per cent socializing or politicking; and
- 18 per cent motivating or reinforcing.

Hence it is clear that managers seem to spend much of their time establishing and maintaining relationships.

The reality of practice in public services organizations may be managers conforming to role expectations ('keeping one's nose clean'), not violating bureaucratic norms and demonstrating loyalty to superiors or their departments. Not enough is known about the motivations of public services managers acting at different levels and in different organizations, nor their values. In evidence to the Nolan Committee, former permanent secretary Sir Peter Kemp (Nolan 1995, para. 966: 194) suggested that: 'I think that people who join the public service join it because they want to join the public service as such. They join it because they want to serve. That's my experience of it. They have some consciousness of what it means in serving the public – a job to be done. I think that the continuation of the desire to serve, that almost ethical view of the thing, will continue'.

We need to consider how the principles of public service are operationalized, as discussed in the previous chapter. This takes place through individuals engaged in relationships expressed through obligation, duty, trust and loyalty. However, we cannot divorce individual motivations from the wider organizational and social conventions within which traditions, organizational memories and training are to be found. Individual acts are given meaning within particular practices. We can condemn individual acts but this is a different order of things than condemning a whole practice. However, it is in small individual acts expressed through a set of relationships that the public service ethos comes to light. The manager gives expression to the ethos through dealing with people in terms of care, diligence, courtesy and integrity. The public service ethos is best perceived through the quality of these face-to-face relationships, through processes as much as results.

The manager is at the centre of a web of relationships which entail obligations and duties that need to be balanced. The multiplicity of different stakeholders in the public services makes the manager's commitments

Table 5.2 OUBS research: how 3 key concepts were perceived to apply to a range of stakeholders

Stakeholder		Concept in order of priority	
	Loyalty	Accountability	Responsiveness
Politicians	7	1	=6
The public at large	6	3	2
Individual clients	5	5	1
Immediate supervisor	4	2	=6
Oneself	3	4	5
Colleagues	1	6	4
Subordinates	2	7	3

even more numerous. However, despite this truism, little work has been done on defining the different forms and limits of these relationships. A civil servant may have loyalties:

- to a professsional body and its professional standards;
- as an employee expected to implement decisions taken by superiors;
- as a servant of the Crown accountable to Parliament through ministers;
- as a public official with a duty to clients;
- as a private individual.

The civil servant may be subject to a number of competing duties and obligations. However, the location of these duties and obligations will be different depending upon the functions performed, the level within the department or relationships with external stakeholders. For example, senior officials in central departments are very much concerned with traditional accountability to the minister and with ensuring that advice remains impartial. Chief executives in those line departments with a commercial role are interested in 'more bang for the buck' and with ensuring that public money is not wasted. Front-line managers are concerned with acting in a proper manner when handing out contracts and are extremely sensitive to accusations of impropriety and corruption.

Managers will also see that different relationships are governed by different requirements. The OUBS survey, referred to in previous chapters, demonstrated where managers believe that loyalty, accountability and responsiveness are located (see Table 5.2).

We can draw three clear conclusions from the survey results:

1 loyalty is seen to apply strongest to immediate colleagues and subordinates i.e. it has an internal focus;
2 accountability is seen, in the first instance, to be upwards in the hierarchy of the organisation;
3 responsiveness is seen to be outwards to clients and the public.

Relationships within the public services are often defined by the employer in terms of performance. The notion of office as a vocation, as described by Kemp (Nolan Committee 1995), appears to have become increasingly outdated. A feature of more traditional relationships has been trust and we will explore this in some detail through the relationship between the minister and the Civil Service in a later section.

The concept of trust

Trust has been defined in a number of ways, for example: 'Trust is based upon an individual's belief as to how another will perform on some future occasion' (Good 1988: 33); '. . . correct expectations about the *actions* of other people that have a bearing on one's own choice of action when that action must be chosen before one can monitor the actions of others' (Dasgupta 1988: 51, original emphasis). In these definitions trust is concerned with relationships with others; it involves expectations about other people's actions. It focuses on the present and the past and has implications for the future. Luhmann (1979) has argued that a major feature of trust is its ability to reduce the complexity of the future – we take things on trust. The ability to reduce an uncertain future is possible within a familiar world. We need to be aware of what has gone on before. In terms of personal relationships it is easier for an individual to place trust in another if the individual has some knowledge of how that person has performed in similar situations before. If a student informs his tutor that his essay will be presented on time the tutor will have difficulty in believing the student if all his previous essays have been handed in late. Trust takes place within a context of past performance. It exists in circumstances where we need to rely upon others. In deciding what action to undertake we need to be able to rely upon the behaviour of others, to have expectations of it. Barber (1983) has indicated that there are three different types of expectation:

1 Those concerned with normal social life and the maintenance of persistence, stability and order.
2 Those that we have of 'technically competent role performance' such that we trust, for example, the surgeon to perform the operation well, or the official to pay out benefits correctly.
3 Those that we have of others to carry out their fiduciary responsibilities and obligations.

Trust performs the function in social, professional or economic life of allowing order, stability, continuity and, indeed, the maintenance of any kind of life at all. Recall the question from Chapter 1, 'What if promises were not kept and we could not rely on others?' Barber (1983: 21) suggests

Table 5.3 Roles and relationships

	Public relationships	*Private relationships*
Expectations	Defined by role	Emerge in the course of mutual interaction
Characteristics	Effectiveness A calculating stance Designed to fit a role	Trust Non-instrumental Grow and develop
Objectives	To achieve predetermined goals	An end in itself

that: 'Trust is an integrative mechanism that creates and sustains solidarity in social relationships and systems'. From this perspective trust manifests itself in terms of relationships and in the maintenance of those relationships. Trust also operates in a number of different contexts and we need to investigate whether or not the relationship in question is professional, personal, economic or institutional. Different obligations and duties to others will arise depending upon how the relationship is perceived. Jones (1984) argues that conflicts arise when individuals see their roles differently. Jones examines the nature of public and private roles and argues that private roles emerge in particular one-to-one relationships and are ends in themselves. He suggests that public roles are designed only to achieve the goal of the organization and no more, whereas private roles grow. Performance in a public role is judged by the extent to which goals are achieved, and the criterion is effectiveness. The attitudes of the individual are irrelevant except in so far as they affect the ability to perform well in the role. This argument is supported by the research carried out by Gabarro (1978) on how managers develop working relationships with their subordinates. Task accomplishment was a central criterion in developing trust with personal liking or attraction relatively unimportant. For Jones (1984) an arms-length calculating stance is regarded as appropriate for performers in public roles and inappropriate for those engaged in private roles. The distinction between the different kinds of role will be blurred and the location of the boundary will change over time. These issues are presented in Table 5.3.

The concept of a public role may be more appropriate in characterizing a relationship of contract rather than sociability or personal relations. A feature of such a relationship will be limited commitment. A contract specifies clearly what obligations and duties are covered whereas a personal relationship is characterized by an open-ended commitment. However, Jones (1984) presupposes that public roles are purely instrumental and amoral in character. We have argued throughout this book that this represents an outdated view of the rational administrator implementing

policies determined by others and that, in fact, the processes and relationships involved are of prime importance. Virtues are important to the
public services manager and we would expect them to consist of treating
stakeholders with respect, dignity, politeness and sensitivity; in fact all the
virtues we expect of our private relationships. As Jos and Hines (1993:
382) argue:

> ... the public service presents employees with moral issues that re-
> quire attributes often associated with our private lives – sensitivity,
> compassion, trustworthiness – as well as those generally regarded as
> appropriate to our public and professional lives – impartiality and
> effective attainment of externally imposed goals. That is, the adminis-
> trative domain is not solely public or private.

What is more important than an artificial distinction between public and
private is a distinction between an economic exchange based on contracts
and a social exchange based on social relations. Even here, an economic
exchange is based on the premise that contracts for the most part will not
be broken. Fox (1974) argues that an economic exchange is similar to that
which is specified in a contract whereas in a social exchange there is an
absence of a specifically defined obligation. Whereas a social exchange
may be characterized by high discretion and high trust, an economic exchange will be characterized by low discretion and low trust.

We also need to be aware of how trust manifests itself. It would not
make sense to suggest that we trusted our doctor if we constantly questioned his or her expertise by seeking other medical opinions. In the same
way, parents cannot be said to trust their teenage children when out with
friends if the parents insist on accompanying their children everywhere.
There would have to be some sign of trust, some evidence that the parent
trusted the teenager to behave as the parent thought appropriate. There
has to be discretion. The manager who constantly watches over a subordinate's work cannot be said to trust that worker to perform to expectations
without the manager's presence. However, we may not expect trust to be
given as a matter of course but rather given in the light of experience.
Presumably, if teenagers show what the parent might consider to be a
mature, responsible attitude to, say, their first party then the parent is
more likely to trust them on subsequent occasions. Trust follows from
particular instances; the patient should not trust the doctor, therefore,
without exception but in the light of the particular relationship that has
built up over time between the doctor and the patient within the context of
general medical practice. We can look for signs of trust and come up with
indicators that show trust. Fox (1974) has suggested that we can distinguish between high and low trust relationships and these can be presented
as shown in Table 5.4. Fox suggests that high trust will characterize a

Table 5.4 Trust and relationships

High trust	Low trust
Participants share goals/values	Participants have divergent goals/values
They have diffuse long-term obligations towards each other	They have short-term specific obligations towards each other
There is open-ended support	The costs and benefits of support are calculated
They communicate openly and honestly	They resist and screen communications
They rely upon each other	They minimize dependence upon each other
They give each other the benefit of the doubt	They are quick to suspect and invoke sanctions on default of obligations

non-instrumental relationship whereas low trust characterizes an instrumental relationship.

Our concern, thus far, has been primarily with trust as a feature of personal relationships and we have identified five characteristics. These are:

1 Expectations about other people are based upon past performance.
2 Relationships will take place within a context of roles.
3 These roles may include social, professional and institutional relationships.
4 Trust enhances order, stability and predictability.
5 Trust requires a commitment by those involved in the relationship.

We also need to consider the relationship between the different parties in terms of equality. Does a trust relationship imply equal participation? Are there mutual obligations and duties arising as a result of the relationship? A social relationship may require an equal commitment by both parties; if let down constantly by a friend then we may come to believe that the relationship is not that important to the friend. The relationship will wane if it is expected that social relationships are about equal commitments and the fulfilling of obligations. In the case of the doctor-patient relationship a different kind of relationship may obtain where it is sufficient that the patient trusts the doctor. In return the patient will anticipate receiving appropriate medical advice and good treatment. The point is that the parties to the exchange may well be motivated by different considerations. We need to be aware of the different kinds of exchange involved. A legal exchange may be more limited than a social exchange where the commitment to a social exchange is more open-ended and may not involve specifically defined duties or obligations. Similarly, an economic exchange may specify duties and obligations in the form of a contract. Neveretheless, in order for such limited exchanges to take place and be successful they will be located within the general context of trust in the economic sytem or legal system to ensure the validity of, and general agreement to, such exchanges.

The content of the minister-civil servant relationship

The concept of trust is at the heart of the relationship between the minister and the civil servant. According to former head of the Civil Service Sir Robert Armstrong (1985: 3) 'Civil servants are under an obligation to keep the confidences to which they become privy in the course of their official duties, not only the maintenance of trust betwen the Ministers and civil servants but also the efficiency of government depend on their so doing'. Traditionally, the relationship has been perceived as the loyal and impartial Civil Service serving the minister to the best of their ability and secure in the knowledge that their advice will be protected from public view (see Ridley 1983). Civil servants are expected to suppress their own political convictions and not to express personal opinions even when called to give evidence (for example, before parliamentary committees). This view has been criticized over the years and it has been suggested that the notion of a departmental ethos shapes the officials' thinking in one direction or another and precludes neutrality; that the role of trade unions within the Civil Service has led to a more overt political stance or that the social and educational background of senior officials represents a slanted perspective on issues of government. Indeed, if neutrality does exist, this may not necessarily be an advantage. In the age of conviction politics that characterized the 1980s, the tradition of neutrality sat uneasily alongside the emphasis on commitment.

However, while commitment may be appropriate for a personal relationship it may not be appropriate for other kinds of relationship. We need to consider to what extent the minister-civil servant relationship can be depicted as a personal relationship. At the same time commitment may not necessarily be political in nature. Former permanent secretary at the Treasury, Sir Douglas Wass (1983: 14), makes the point that 'No one would argue that the professional detachment of the practising solicitor implied any lack of commitment to the client's interests'.

A further feature of the relationship is that of loyalty. The convention in British politics has been of loyalty first and foremost to the minister in charge of the department. This tradition was confirmed in Sir Robert Armstrong's memorandum (Armstrong 1985) to the Civil Service following the trial and acquittal of Clive Ponting. Armstrong, at the time head of the Civil Service and Cabinet secretary, issued a memorandum to the effect that the foremost duty of the civil servant is to the Crown which 'for all practical purposes is represented by the government of the day' (Armstrong 1985: 1). Evidence given to the Treasury and Civil Service Committee (1986) which examined the duties of civil servants and their relationships with ministers was critical of the Armstrong line and expressed the view that the Crown was something more enduring than the government of the day. At the same time, as we have already seen, there may be other loyalties commanding the attention of the civil servant. However, one commentator has suggested that because appraisals and promotion are in the hands of more senior civil servants, '. . . when it is a question of loyalties, any civil servant knows where his bread is buttered and how to get at the jam' (Crowther Hunt 1980: 393).

Heclo and Wildavsky (1981) point to the importance of the trust between officials in the village community that characterizes Whitehall and which is not available to the politician. In any relationship, for it to be sustained over time, we would expect loyalty to flow from both participants. Ministerial loyalty may be expressed in terms of public praise by the minister for the work of officials or springing to their defence when attacked. However, in recent times, it has not been considered necessary to defend public services, and the abolition of trade unions, in 1984, for some categories of workers at the government communication centre GCHQ suggested that the government did not believe in the loyalty of some of its officials. The prime minister at the time, Margaret Thatcher, argued that union membership was incompatible with national loyalty. Likewise during the Westland affair (1986) the Secretary of State for Defence, Michael Heseltine, and the Secretary of State for Trade and Industry, Leon Brittan, openly disagreed about a strategy for putting together a rescue package for Westland which was the only British company manufacturing helicopters for military purposes. The Select Committee was critical of Leon Brittan for mobilizing his officials at the Department of Trade and Industry to disseminate information and then not supporting them. Trust is a delicate flower and needs nurturing. The present Labour government has proposed to bring in outside policy advisers and its decision not to allow civil servants to participate in the final drafting of a White Paper on a freedom of information bill (because of suggestions that it might be 'nobbled') is not guaranteed to smooth ruffled feathers (see the *Observer* newspaper, 13 July 1997).

The possibility exists that different parties to the minister-civil servant relationship will see that relationship in different ways and come to have different expectations of the relationship. Not only that but it may be possible for the minister to know personally the members of the senior Civil Service but it is unlikely that he or she will have a personal relationship with many other civil servants. Ministerial personal influence may not percolate that far down a department.

The limits of the trust relationship

It has not until recently been thought necessary to specify clearly the limits to or the precise guidelines for the relationship between ministers and their civil servants. That relationship has been governed by traditions, customs and conventions. From John Locke (1632–1704) onwards, the proper limits of government activity has continued to be a part of the debate of liberal democratic government. The concept of trust is crucial to Locke's account of the relationship between the state and the citizen such that when the limits set to guide that relationship are transgressed, trust is broken. For Locke, ultimately the citizens have a right to revolt and to freedom from interference by government (see Locke, *Of Government*).

While revolt might seem a fairly drastic measure for civil servants to take, we are concerned with the limits to the relationship, with what can legitimately be asked of civil servants by ministers. The civil servant may ask 'Does the minister have the right to ask this or that of me?' In recent times the Ponting case highlighted this issue when Clive Ponting argued that a civil servant must ultimately place loyalty to Parliament and the public interest above obligation to the government of the day. The views of Justice McCowan and Sir Robert Armstrong (1985) were that the interests of the state are synonymous with the interests of the government of the day. This is in contrast to the Civil Service code of ethics in the USA which stipulates that loyalty is owed foremost to the highest moral principles rather than to a party or government department.

When custom and convention no longer appear to work, then the immediate call is to state explicitly the limits and content of relationships that have been previously taken on trust. This was recognized in the report of the Treasury and Civil Service Committee (1986: para. 3.12): 'The continuing uncertainty and lack of agreement on the mutual relationship between Ministers and civil servants is a major factor in the current malaise'. The appropriate characterization of the relationship between the minister and the civil servant may be one that involves a contractual exchange and is best expressed in clear and formal codes of conduct.

The context of the trust relationship

So far we have asssumed that trust relationships are between individuals. Does it make sense to discuss the notion of trusting an institution or a group? For example, are all doctors to be trusted or just the individual doctors with whom we enter into a specific relationship? Presumably it will depend in part upon the reputation of doctors as a group and their professional ethic. Thus, part of the *context* of a relationship will be that of group norms and reputations; these will form part of the background. We expect doctors to be concerned, first and foremost, with the welfare of their patients. There will be general condemnation if a doctor does not place the interests of the patient first. There may well then be a specific relationship within a general context. Relationships will change depending upon the context; problems arise when the context of the relationship has changed but one party does not recognize the change. The official may come to be suspicious of a minister who seeks alternative sources of advice, or exposes the official to public scrutiny or wishes the official to express a partisan political commitment to government. Indeed senior officials expressed disquiet at the role that Bernard Ingham played for Margaret Thatcher given that the prime minister's press secretary is considered to be an impartial civil servant. More recently, the current head of the Civil Service, Sir Robin Butler, blocked an attempt by John Major and Michael Heseltine to instruct civil servants to find government contractors willing to endorse the Conservative Party in the run-up to the 1997 general election. There appears to be a growing recognition that there may be a fusion at the centre of government such that the distinction between the politician and the administrator has become increasingly blurred. We make no comment on whether this is a good thing or not but merely outline the implications for their relationship. In the Seventh Report from the Treasury and Civil Service Committee (1986), many witnesses doubted the wisdom of Robert Armstrong's reiteration of the views of Sir Warren Fisher on the role of the Civil Service. The FDA expressed the view that their members '... were looking for some suggestion that the world had changed and when they did not get it they were disappointed' (para. 2.4).

From high trust to low trust?

To what extent has the changing relationship between the politician and the administrator resulted in a loss of confidence or lack of trust in either party? Traditionally the reputation of Civil Service virtues has led to expressions of trust in its performance by all political parties. More recently the Civil Service has been seen as a scapegoat for poor economic performance and its status, prestige and privileges have come under scrutiny, particularly by governments that have been committed to 'rolling back the frontiers of the state'. Indeed, on coming to power in 1979, Margaret Thatcher seemed determined to undermine the position of the Civil Service as a whole. What implications did this have for our concept of trust?

Mutual trust will require reciprocal adherence to existing arrangements or agreements to change those arrangements provided that both sides have incentives to do so. Did the existing conventions and 'rules of the game' delineating minister-civil servant relationships break down? Apart from the Westland affair, GCHQ and Ponting, other issues involved the reduction in the number of civil servants from approximately 740,000 in 1979 to 500,000 in 1997, the abrogation of existing mechanisms for determining pay, the use of outsiders, short-term contracts and so on, all of which might be seen to undermine the role of the Civil Service. At the same time there have been Civil Service strikes and a flow of leaks from civil servants. Put this alongside the view held by some politicians that the Civil Service employs delaying tactics, forecloses options, slants statistics and interprets policy decisions in ways not intended, and it all adds up to mutual distrust and suspicion.

To what extent, though, does it matter what the relationship is between the minister and the civil servant and how important would a decline in trust be? Ridley (1987: 85) makes the point that:

> Leaks are, of course likely to reduce trust, but we have no real evidence about the extent to which an occasional leak in exceptional circumstances would seriously undermine ministerial confidence in the service as a whole. Has whistle-blower legislation led to a dangerous decline of confidence in the Amercian civil service? Does the survival of organisations, indeed, depend on absolute trust between members?

A perceived decline in trust may not lead to a crisis; it depends upon who or what is involved. A decline in trust in individual politicians, as we have seen recently in the UK, may not matter too much for the continuity of the system in much the same way as a decline in trust of an individual doctor may have no effect on continuing trust in the medical profession as a whole.

We need to clarify the relationship between the minister and the senior civil servant. Is it the same kind of relationship that the minister will have with other civil servants in the department? Next Steps Agencies introduced framework agreements between the Agency and the minister which specified responsibilities, and such a development may solve the problem of the all-embracing nature of the convention of ministerial responsibility. However, the sacking of Derek Lewis as head of the Prisons Agency by the then home secretary, Michael Howard, left senior officials condemning the minister for transgressing rules specifying constitutional obligations.

The fragmentation of central government has created different types of officials with different relationships with government. The first head of Margaret Thatcher's policy unit, John Hoskyns, was scathing of the traditions of the Civil Service. According to Hoskyns, dispassionate detachment needs to be replaced by energy and enthusiasm, characteristics that are more likely to be found in political appointees than in career officials. A general commitment on the part of officials to their minister rather than specific obligations or duties formally laid down in some kind of contract is said to be part of the tradition of the Civil Service but may no longer be appropriate. It may well be that in the 1980s and 1990s the relationship has moved from high trust to low trust. Ministers and civil servants appear to have divergent goals and values. Given the different roles and the length of time in office of ministers, there are short-term obligations towards each other rather than a long-term commitment. Rather than open-ended support for each other, costs and benefits are traded off. Communications are screened and limited rather than open and honest and the dependence upon each other are minimized. The use of outside advisers are a manifestation of this. Do ministers and civil servants give each other the benefit of the doubt? Civil servants will wonder at the motives of a minister who asks them to leak information and the minister may suspect the motives of an official who argues that they have a duty to some conception of the public interest which overrides their loyalty to the minister.

By using the concept of trust generations of civil servants have projected an image of their relationship with ministers that has all the attributes of a personal relationship but is no longer convincing. The concept of a personal relationship may no longer be appropriate and we should recognize that the appropriate characterization is one that involves a contractual exchange. Such an exchange would require clear guidelines for both parties to that exchange and would require a commitment by both parties to follow those guidelines. Thus a set of standard expectations fixed in advance would follow from these. Obligations and duties would be specified and, as with a trust relationship, order, stability and predictability would be ensured. A code of written guidelines would have these advantages. Such guidelines would recognize the ethical dimensions to the relationship. Since both ministers and civil servants would need to be committed to these guidelines both parties would be involved in deciding what they would consist of and what the limits were. Where disagreements occurred as to the precise limits of the guidelines an independent arbitrator could resolve the dispute.

Such guidelines would be subject to regular review in the light of changing circumstances to overcome the danger of ossification but if both parties are committed to continuing the relationship then such reviews will be seen as part of that commitment. At the very least the disquiet found since the early 1980s would be replaced by clear expectations of the other party's role which is, after all, at the heart of the relationship of trust.

In fact the Civil Service code, first proposed in *Taking Forward Continuity and Change* (Cabinet Office 1995), specifies the duty of ministers towards civil servants and included giving due consideration to the advice offered by civil servants. Ministers were also required not to ask civil servants to carry out tasks that may be in breach of the proposed code. The Questions of Procedure for Ministers (Cabinet Office 1992, para. 27) requires that: 'Each Minister is responsible to Parliament for the conduct of his or her department, and for the actions carried out by the department in pursuit of government policies or in the discharge of responsibilities laid upon him or her as a Minister'. (See Hennessy 1996 for a full discussion of QPM including the Nolan Committee's 1995 view on the Procedures.) For their part, civil servants were also required to conduct themselves in such a way as to retain ministerial trust. However, trust once lost is hard to regain, and the whole issue will require sensitive handling by the new government.

Professional relationships and trust

This chapter has focused on relationships between ministers and civil servants as a device for exploring in some detail the nature of the trust relationship. As we indicated in the introduction to the chapter there is a host of other relationships that are part of delivering public services and we now turn to a brief examination of these.

As we noticed in the introduction, asymmetric information can exist between a principal and the agent and professional relations are often characterized by such inequalities in information. The problem is where one side uses the power that can emerge out of unequal dependencies. This is where trust comes in; we have to trust professionals because we do not have the expertise to judge the rightness or wrongness of their judgements. As Dawson (1994: 145) puts it: 'The relationship between a professional and a client is necessarily an unequal one. This difference in knowledge and experience of the two parties requires a great deal of trust to be placed in the professional by the client'. That trust is generated by the professional ethos. According to Lebacqz (1985), professionalism includes:

- A sense of calling or commitment.
- Using knowledge and skill to provide an 'objective' diagnosis of problems.
- A need to cooperate with colleagues.
- A requirement of confidentality towards the client.
- The notion that service is primary, remuneration is secondary.
- Continuing education and skills.
- Sensitivity to client rights and well-being.
- An affirmation of good citizenship.

The role of professionals in the welfare state is considerable, not least because some 30 per cent of professionals work in the public services. However, Bertilsson (1990) identifies professionals as the mediators betweeen the state and the citizen in terms of welfare legislation. Wrigley and McKevitt (1994: 78) argue that professionals provide a dual role, acting on behalf of the state but also as an agent of the client:

The need to ration the service at an operational level is a major factor that makes the activities of professionals in core public services quite different to those of the professionals in business firms in the market system. It is professional judgement not customer affluence which largely determines the allocation of resources within the areas of health, education and welfare. But of course, professionals' judgement can be affected by many factors, including fear of malpractice suits, difficulty in coping with political pressures, as well, of course, as assessment of what the client really needs.

Increasingly, as McKevitt and Lawton (1996) argue, professionals may be seeking to hold the line between pressures for cost containment and emerging evidence of a decline in service quality. Indeed, Travers (1993: 46) argues that the professionalism of those working in local government allowed reforms to take place even though it could be argued that many of the reforms were not in their best interest:

> Senior officers in most council departments have used their professional competence to ensure that externally-imposed changes have been introduced without service breakdowns, and, in many cases, within severe financial constraints. Initial training, codes of conduct, career development and the basic integrity of local government accountants, lawyers and service chiefs have ensured that non-partisan professional standards have been maintained.

However, it is worth pointing out that there are different forms of professional relationship. One type of professional relationship is characterized by obligations to patients or clients and this is how professionals define their role. It is not just about possessing technical competence but engaging in a role that incurs obligations and duties, primarily to individuals. Another type of professional relationship relies upon technical competence and the presentation of information based upon that expertise. We might think of lawyers, accountants, or engineers in this light whose prime focus might be internal to the organization rather than outwards to clients. Stoker (1993, see pp. 6–8) has identified five types of professionals that have developed under the new local government regime:

1 The de-skilled professional such as librarians whose traditional skills have been replaced by new technology.
2 The constrained professional, suffering from the imposition of national controls such as the National Curriculum for teachers. Stoker describes this as a 'shading of autonomy' (p. 6).
3 The contracting professional, working at arms-length on a contractual basis such as housing managers, as a result of changes in the delivery of services.

4 The technocrat professional offering new business skills.
5 The managerial professional, determined to deliver organizational performance and possessing management qualifications.

According to Stoker, all five can exist within the same profession.

Different professionals will engage with each other and with their clients at different levels. A front-line social worker may have more in common with their health service counterpart than with the director of social services. It is often the case that professionals working at the front line do not have the same problems over jurisdiction than their superiors might have. While senior managers in the differing caring services may disagree with each other over who has responsibility, or what kind of service is to be provided or who is to fund it, social workers and health workers will work together to produce the best service for the client or the patient.

However, professionals have come under increasing attack. At one level their autonomy and self-regulation has been under attack from those critics who argue that professionals have too much power and act in their own interest rather than that of their clients. The professional ethos is seen to cloak self-interest. Increasingly professionals have also come under attack from those who argue that managerial decisions, made in the light of the citizen body as a whole rather than the individual client, should be given priority. Indeed, critics of managerialism such as Pollitt (1993) believe that power has shifted to managers rather than professionals. Professional-managerial relationships can lead to conflict: 'Controls other than self controls are needed to protect the organization from the potential profligacy of professionals and their occasionally myopic belief in their own and their professions' overriding importance' (Lee and Piper 1988: 124).

The justification of management interference may depend upon their acquisition of the requisite skills; in local government this may not be much of a problem since senior managers tend to come up through the professional route. Management may employ the discourse of the sovereign consumer to justify further inroads into professional autonomy. Has there been a shift of balance away from the producer to the consumer? As we argued above, the professional may in fact be holding the line. At the same time, power may be transferred from one group of professionals to another; for example, fundholding GPs now act on behalf of the patient as purchasers. The patient only has power by proxy – it is the GP who has benefited.

There are a number of potential tensions in the relationship between managers and professionals:

- Freedom to manage is a direct challenge to the freedom of professionals.
- Central controls through performance measures go against professional autonomy.
- The rhetoric of the consumer takes power away from the professional.

- Managers look after the interests of the organization as a whole; the professional concentrates on the individual.
- Competition may inhibit professional collaboration.

Yet the medical profession, for example, still has tremendous power. According to Harrison and Pollitt (1994) there are a number of reasons why further growth in the power of managers in the NHS may be constrained:

- The existing power of professional groups.
- Managers increasing dependence for finance from private patients which means relying on doctors.
- New contractual arrangements mean increasing opportunity to move away from managerial hierarchies.
- It is not in the managers interest to seek control in some areas – rationing decisions are controversial.
- Institutions of management are likely to become fragmented and it is an assumption that managers speak with one voice.
- In the long run government will not escape political pressure.
- Consumer empowerment may begin to challenge the dominance of the manager.

At another level professionals have been criticized for putting professional ethics before individual morality. The confidentiality of client information is supposed to override any other considerations but what if that information relates to some wrongdoing? Judgement can be suspended as professionals hide behind their role. Personal responsibilty should not be abrogated.

In contrast to the professional, the manager is at the heart of a set of relationships with different stakeholders. In so far as these stakeholders are individuals, groups or the community, they all represent different ways of seeing the world. The management skill is in reconciling these different viewpoints, particularly in those services which require cross-boundary working. In the domestic arena, community care means that people with different views reflecting, among others, a health or a social care perspective, have to be reconciled. Managing in a multicultural environment is a reality for the modern manager.

Managing across organizational boundaries and partnerships

Public services are increasingly delivered through a network of organizations and involve joint working and partnerships. Such developments involve managers in acquiring new skills such as contract management, and new relationships between organizations. One of these new relationships takes an economic form and Williamson (1975) offers us an analysis of such an approach. He asks under what conditions economic functions are best performed within the firm or best performed outside the firm through market forces. He proposes that transactions are more likely to take place within firms when those transactions:

- are uncertain in outcome;
- recur frequently;
- require transaction-specific investments (time, money or energy which cannot be easily transferred to other types of interaction);
- are characterized by bounded rationality, defined as the difficulty in specifying all contingencies, and by opportunism – the possibility of one party cheating.

At the same time, exchange in the open market is the best for transactions which:

- are straightforward;
- are non-repetitive;
- require no transaction-specific investment.

In deciding whether or not to contract out a service, a public sector organization may wish to consider how easily available in the marketplace are specialist skills and knowledge; how easy it is to write contracts that cover all eventualities; whether internal efficiency can be improved; how important continuity of service is; and how much control can be exercised over external agencies.

Managers are increasingly having to manage across organizational boundaries. And yet management *by contracts* may not always be the most appropriate relationship between and within organizations. Tightly specified contracts will be inappropriate where there is a lack of perfect information or the environment is uncertain. At the same time, to replace an informal relationship that has worked well with a tightly specified contract may undermine existing trust. However, as governments are increasingly faced with problems that cut across organizational and professional boundaries, the ability of individual units to achieve their own objectives will increasingly depend not just on their own decisions but on those of other organizations. Managers increasingly manage in networks and partnerships which require different skills and have different ethical implications. Such relationships involve not just two parties or agencies but a multitude of different agencies and thus need:

> a more problematic model, derived from interorganizational theory, which sees the centre-to-periphery system as a network of actors, each with its own autonomy derived from different sources, through which the final outcome is unlikely to correspond to legislative intention. Reciprocity and bargaining rather than hierarchy thus describe the way the service delivery system functions.
>
> (Sharpe 1985: 380)

Network relations are more complex than a two-way flow of information or consultation. A network is a set of relationships that exist at different levels within and across organizations. These relationships may be between individuals or groups, will change over time and will involve both formal and informal relationships. Increasingly, public services managers are being encouraged to look outward to customers, clients or citizens and to engage in activities with the local community. Managing such networks requires four main skills:

1 Managing across jurisdictions. Managers will need to manage the interests of their own organization and those of the network as a whole. The manager will need to recognize that members of the network within the public services may represent separate and distinct legal entities with different systems of accountability.
2 Managing different stakeholders. This means recognizing that different interests need to be balanced. Common interests will need to be identified and conflicting interests reconciled. It means enforcing commitments across organizational boundaries.
3 Managing implementation. This will entail coordinating the different groups involved and developing appropriate structures and mechanisms for effective implementation. It will also mean generating information, respecting confidences and building trust. If trust and goodwill do not exist then joint venture agreements specifying the rights and obligations of the different parties may have to be signed.
4 Managing incrementally. This is concerned with bargaining and negotiation in which different parties seek to maximize their gains through negotiation and mutual accommodation, and with avoiding mutually damaging behaviour.

Much of the delivery of public services requires managing across organizational boundaries whether it be in terms of community care, child protection, or economic development. For successful policy implementation the dangers to be avoided include:

- Not considering the views of all the stakeholders nor their perceptions, e.g. taking a medical diagnosis as the only diagnosis and not recognizing that there may be, for example, a social care diagnosis.
- Lack of clarity of objectives.
- Entrenched positions.
- Lack of mutual accommodation.
- Avoiding territorial and professional boundaries.
- Not allowing equal access to key stakeholders.
- Not understanding or having sympathy with the roles of others.
- Not recognizing that different organizational cultures and values have to be considered.

Underpinning this is a belief in the importance and relevance of the views of all relevant stakeholders and a belief in participation in the policy process. Kernaghan (1993b) has argued that power sharing is similar to empowerment and reflects the citizen partnership models of the 1970s. A true partnership is empowering: '. . . a partnership . . . is a relationship involving the sharing of power, work, support and/or information with others for the achievement of joint goals and/or mutual benefits' (Kernaghan 1993b: 61).

The ethics of partnerships, then, are concerned with power; professional relationships are one-to-one. Now the argument is that there is a multiplicity of relationships which undermine the power of the professionals. This is a crucial development and may be seen to undermine professional autonomy – it is a hard lesson for professionals to learn! However, effective partnerships require:

- a foundation of common values;
- shared vision;
- effective communication;
- a tradition of joint working such that trust has had time to develop.

Kernaghan (1993b: 73–5) offer six features of a successful partnership:

1 It must include all relevant stakeholders whose contribution is necessary for the achievement of goals.
2 The greater the degree of mutual dependence the greater the chance of success.
3 The greater the extent to which participants are empowered the more chance there is that the partnership will be effective and enduring.
4 The pooling of resources will create a synergy which is greater than the sum of the individual parts.
5 A partnership with limited objectives has more chance of success than one with broad aims.
6 The more formalized a partnership is, the more likely it is to be sustained; accountability can be specified.

Rules and rule-governed behaviour

Individuals' behaviour within organizations is subject to rules and regulations, both formal and informal. Within any organization there will be informal rules that guide behaviour and there will be sanctions, both formal and informal, that are invoked. Peer pressure is an important social constraint. For informal rules to be effective they need to be internalized by those who are bound by them. A more formal approach is provided by codes of conduct, which are becoming increasingly common in both public and private sector organizations.

Individuals working in organizations operate within systems of rules, both formal and informal, which perform a number of different functions. Formal rules can ensure consistency, continuity, control and accountability. Informal rules might aid in the functioning of organizations by developing an organizational culture perhaps expressed as 'the way we do things around here', establishing customs and developing harmonious relationships. Sometimes, however, compliance with rules becomes an overriding consideration so that the existence of a rule becomes an excuse for not thinking or for suspending critical judgement. Employees can get worn down by too many rules which appear to erect barriers to achieving objectives. Staff may take short cuts or bypass procedures; a manager may not take up references for awarding contracts or offering an applicant a job; a manager may give out grants because the group or individual is deserving enough even though they may not appear to fit the criteria or specified category for that particular grant. Good intentions may lead to problems if, for example, a job applicant has been 'economical with the truth'. It is worth remembering that rules do have a purpose and that they can guide behaviour as well as constrain it. One way of regulating behaviour within organizations is through codes of conduct. Codes of conduct can take different forms and be concerned with professional ethics as determined by a professional body which concentrates on individual behaviour, or with organizational codes such as company codes which more and more organizations are using. Many professions do have their own codes which serve to regulate the relationship between the client and the professional. This relationship is, as we have discussed, necessarily an unequal one requiring a great deal of trust. The client may need some guarantee that he or she is being treated with due professional care and attention and that sanctions can be invoked where this is lacking. Professional codes may serve a number of purposes:

- The promotion of ethical behaviour and the deterrence of unethical behaviour.
- The provision of a set of standards, a written benchmark against which to judge behaviour.
- To act as guidance when faced with difficult decisions.
- The establishment of rights and responsibilities.
- Provide a statement of principles indicating what the profession stands for.
- The creation of a contract between professionals and their clients.
- A statement of professional development.
- The legitimation of professional norms and the justification for sanctions when those norms are ignored or unethical conduct occurs.
- The enhancement of the status of the profession.
- A statement of professional conduct, identifying client expectations.

A code can function as a public statement of ethical principles and informs others of what to expect. Codes can take various forms. Kernaghan (1975) identified codes as lying between a continuum of, at one end a 'Ten Commandments' approach which includes a general statement of broad ethical principles without any provision for monitoring or enforcement, and at the other end what Kernaghan called the Justinian Code approach which represents a comprehensive and detailed coverage of both principles and administrative arrangements. Most codes will combine elements of both.

We need to ask a number of general questions concerning codes of conduct. First, who draws them up and to what extent do they only reflect the views of the 'code maker'? Second, what function do they perform? As we saw with the description of professional codes above, codes can fulfil a number of functions which will include acting as a guide to conduct, regulating behaviour, providing a set of standards, identifying principles and values, offering a means to resolve dilemmas and so on. Codes can provide independent and predetermined criteria which are written down and can be consulted so as to avoid ambiguity and misunderstanding.

Third, what do codes of conduct consist of? They may range from the comprehensive to the minimal. In UK local government for example, codes for both officers and politicians are fairly comprehensive, covering: the law; standards; disclosure of information; relationships between councillors, officers, the local community, service users and contractors; employment matters; outside commitments of officers; personal interests; equality issues; corruption; use of financial interests; hospitality; sponsorship and so on. (See Third Nolan Report, Nolan Committee 1997; Local Government Management Board, undated). In general terms, many codes are concerned with relations between different groups of stakeholders, financial interests, personal behaviour, the use of official information, duties and responsibilities, public interest and private gain.

Fourth, who do codes of conduct apply to and when? Are they internally focused on the behaviour of managers or do they include an external dimension? It is interesting to note that many private sector organizations now include some statement of corporate social responsibility to the wider community as part of their mission statements. Fifth, are they necessary and do they make a difference? The need for codes is not always recognized, as Box 5.1 indicates.

It is instructive to compare the use of codes with the private sector. Schlegelmilch and Houston (1999: 39) defined a code of conduct as: 'A statement setting down corporate principles, ethics, rules of conduct, codes of practice or company philosophy concerning responsibility to employees, shareholders, consumers, the environment or any other aspects of society external to the company'. As part of their 1988 research they mailed 200 of the largest UK companies with a questionnaire from which 98 replied

---

Box 5.1 Ethics code launch upsets police union (headline in the *Guardian* newspaper, 1 December 1992)

A statement on ethical principles for police officers aimed at responding to criticism and 'changing the culture' of the police was launched in December 1992. The 11-point draft statement, the first of its kind, was intended to 'provide guidance to members of the service when facing difficult moral choices'. The statement was drawn up by the police ethics working party which included representatives of police staff associations and members of the Home Office. The principles enshrined in the statement indicated that police officers should:

1 act with fairness and carry out responsibilities with integrity and impartiality;
2 perform duties with diligence and the proper use of discretion;
3 display self-control, tolerance, understanding and courtesy when dealing with individuals;
4 uphold fundamental human rights displaying respect and compassion to individuals;
5 support colleagues and draw attention to any malpractices;
6 respect the fact that much information required is confidential;
7 exercise force only when justified and use the minimum necessary;
8 act only within the law;
9 use resources to the maximum benefit of the public;
10 accept responsibility for self-development and seek to improve ways of serving the community;
11 accept personal responsibility for acts and omissions.

Critics within the police force argued that existing discipline codes rendered the code of ethics superfluous. Many officers had already been following such principles. It is interesting to note that senior management saw the codes as a chance to change the culture of the organization as well as providing guidance.

(49 per cent) with 74 (37 per cent) actually completing the questionnaire. Reasons given for not completing the questionnaire included lack of time and company policy. However, the researchers found that 42 per cent had introduced a code and these codes were concerned with:

- employee conduct such as insider dealing, confidentiality and the acceptance of gifts (100%);
- community and environmental interests (65%);
- customer service and product quality (58%);
- shareholders return on investment (39%);
- suppliers and contractors (23%);
- political interests (13%);
- innovation and technology (6%).

The main reasons given for the introduction of codes included clarifying and defining policy and conveying this message to various groups. The reasons for not introducing a code included the arguments that they are too broad to be of use, that the issues are covered in other documents, and that they have little relevance in a British context where the existing management culture was deemed to be sufficient to ensure ethical behaviour. It was argued that a corporate philosophy and a natural integrity are already enshrined in British business!

Robertson and Schlegelmilch (1993) identify the use of codes in US firms from the 1970s onwards. In the UK, their existence is a more recent phenomenon. Robertson and Schlegelmilch perceive a corporate code of ethics as occupying the middle ground between the law and internalized social values. In the USA they found that the two most important issues in codes of conduct are associated with employee behaviour that will harm the firm. In the UK, codes have more to do with external constituencies – the customer and the environment: 'Our findings indicate some important differences between US and UK firms in their approaches to ethical issues. The three most striking differences occur in the means of communicating ethics policies, in perceptions of what are important ethical issues, and in the ethical issues adressed in ethics policies and training' (Robertson and Schlegelmilch 1993: 310–11).

UK companies are more likely to communicate ethics policies through senior executives, whereas US companies tend to rely more on their human resources and legal departments. US firms, according to Robertson and Schlegelmilch (1993), consider most ethical issues more important than their UK counterparts.

Finally, in research carried out in Australia by Soutar *et al.* (1995), their 1990 survey of 106 companies listed on the Western Australian Stock Exchange reported four reasons for *not* institutionalizing ethical principles:

1 The company is ethical enough already (55%).
2 The company is too small to need it (30%).
3 There is not enough time to draw up codes (21%).
4 There is a lack of financial resources (11%).

The seven most important reasons for institutionalizing ethics were found to be:

1 To provide employees with guidelines (77%).
2 To be a socially responsible company (69%).
3 To improve the company's public image (69%).
4 To improve management (63%).
5 To establish a better corporate culture (59%).
6 To comply with government guidelines (33%).
7 To reduce white-collar crime (18%).

Motivational factors for compliance were found to be the internalization of ethical norms, compliance with rules and external perceptions. Having an impact upon codes were found to be the ethics of individual managers, the informal influences in the work environment which impact upon ethical behaviour and the formal institutionalization of ethics in the organization.

However, there are a number of powerful critiques of codes of conduct:

- Codes can provide a false sense of security. When faced with a decision it is too easy to refer to a code of conduct; if the issue is covered by a code then don't engage in the activity, if it isn't, then fine.
- Codes cannot be comprehensive enough to cover all eventualities; at some point critical judgement must come into play.
- Codes are often vague and generalized; the hard-pressed manager may want guidance in a particular instance for a particular issue.
- Codes can minimize the responsibility of the individual and act as a shield behind which individuals can hide.
- Codes may also act to protect the profession or the organization from public criticism.
- Powerful interests may be responsible for drawing up the code and enforcing it, and the interests of the weakest stakeholders may not be protected.
- Codes may be ineffective in dealing with systemic corruption.
- Self-regulation, which is encouraged through the adoption of codes, may not be the best way of ensuring that the interests of clients, customers and citizens are protected. The system of internal regulation by professional bodies has revealed little in the way of consistent disbarment of members for breaking a code.
- Codes may reflect one viewpoint, one set of values, and this assumes that the organization is homogeneous. There is the possibility, as we discuss in the next chapter, of different cultures existing within the same organization.

Conclusion

To return to an earlier discussion, ethics is concerned with establishing principles as guides to right action. As we have argued, it does not necessarily follow that a moral action will result. According to Dawson (1994) virtue is required which means the disposition to apply the right principle when required. A code of conduct is an 'outside in' way of looking at issues. Another view is 'inside out' which involves the notion that right conduct follows on from a person being virtuous in the first place (Aristotle's view) rather than applying the appropriate principle in the appropriate circumstances. Dawson uses Wittgenstein's (1953) concept of following a rule to examine the nature of codes of conduct, where following a rule correctly such as, for example, reading a timetable is never enough. Understanding the rules is sometimes problematic and Wittgenstein distinguishes between 'knowing that' and 'knowing how'. We may know that $2 + 2 = 4$ but do we know how? Dawson (1994: 150) argues that: 'A judgement over what action to perform is not a weighting of different possibilities or relevant factors, but a "perception" that something must be done'.

We agree with Kernaghan (1993a) who argues that written codes are an important but insufficient means of promoting public service ethics. How ethical issues are internalized is crucial. Professional socialization can play an important role where it becomes second nature to put the interests of the client first. Not to do so would appear odd in some way. High profile issues such as those involved with corruption or conflicts of interest are only a small part of the field. Kernaghan argues that the role models offered by senior managers and education and training are important. Ethical training is discussed in Chapter 8.

The Third Nolan Report (Nolan Committee 1997) proposes an ethical framework for local government which makes use of the courts and proposes the creation of new tribunals and a new Standards Committee. The Report offers a 'best practice' code which argues that:

- codes should be short, clear statements of principles, not rule books;
- the organisation within which a code operates should have an important role in revising it, or adapting a model to its own needs;
- sanctions should be clear, appropriate, and consistent;
- there should be a firm commitment to educating and training people in the code so that they understand why it is there as well as what it says.

(para. 55: 17)

six

The organizational dimension

Key issues

- The extent to which there is an ethical dimension to organizational purposes.
- How culture and traditions build the ethical fabric of organizations.
- The ethical relationship between an organization and its staff.

Introduction

This chapter focuses upon the organization and the impact that organizational demands have upon the manager. These demands will reflect the purposes for which organizations are constituted, what they are designed to achieve, and how they utilize organizational resources (including people, technology, and structures) to achieve their purposes. At one level we might say that there is a clear distinction between private sector and public sector organizations; the former are designed to make a profit, increase value to stakeholders or increase market share, all of which reflect a financial outcome. On the other hand we might suggest that public service organizations are there to serve citizens in some capacity or another. Such a distinction is too simplistic, as we suggested in Chapter 1. However, the goals of public service organizations will reflect wider societal values. It goes without saying that the 1980s saw a fundamental rethink of the role of the state and a reassessment of the 'proper' role of government. Whatever the limits drawn around government activity, it will still reflect an ethical base.

Even economic arguments for a minimal role of the state will be grounded in ethics. (See the argument for public goods as discussed in Chapter 1, page 13, which relies on some concept of utilitarianism.)

However, all organizations will reflect the values, sometimes ethical, of the wider society. Thus, for example, Fukuyama (1995) argues that trust is crucial to the effective running of society and organizations. You will recall that we examined trust in terms of individual relationships in the previous chapter. Trust in society arises as a result of shared values based around a notion of social capital which is defined as the ability of people to work together for common purposes in groups and organizations. For Fukuyama: 'Trust is the expectation that arises within a community of regular, honest and co-operative behavior, based on commonly shared norms, on the part of other members of that community' (p. 26).

According to Fukuyama (1995) widespread distrust puts a kind of tax on economic activity. At the same time, he argues that there are three paths to sociability – which is essential for economic well-being:

1 Sociability based upon family and kinship.
2 Sociability based upon voluntary associations outside kinship such as schools, clubs etc.
3 Sociability via the state.

Where social capital is highest there will be the most prosperity. Fukuyama (1995: 151) quotes with approval the distinguished economist, Kenneth Arrow (1974: 23):

Now trust has a very important pragmatic value, if nothing else. Trust is an important lubricant of a social system. It is extremely efficient; it saves a lot of trouble to have a fair degree of reliance on other people's word. Unfortunately this is not a commodity which can be bought very easily. If you have to buy it, you already have some doubts about what you've bought. Trust and similar values, loyalty or truth-telling, are examples of what the economist would call 'externalities'. They are goods, they are commodities; they have real, practical, economic value; they increase the efficiency of the system, enable you to produce more goods or more of whatever values you hold in high esteem. But they are not commodities for which trade on the open market is technically possible or even meaningful.

An ethical framework reflects, and is reflected in, political, social and economic environments. It does not matter how extensive state activity is, an ethical framework will exist. What is deemed acceptable behaviour in political, social or economic life will be based upon some notion of fairness, equity, justice, duty or obligations. Of course these notions are not static and will change over time and between different countries with different political, religious, economic and social contexts. There is a constant interplay between the personal, the economic and the social and, as Fukuyama (1995) has argued, this will depend upon concepts such as trust which act as a bedrock for political, social and economic life.

Jabbra and Jabbra (1983) illustrate the relationship between public service organizations and the wider environment. They argue that we need to understand traditional societies in terms of loyalty to kin and tribe; often government is the main employer and it is not therefore unusual to find bribery, favouritism and nepotism. In some societies uneducated citizens are unaware of the public services due to them as a matter of right. Officials encourage the view that the provision of services is a personal favour that they are bestowing and should be rewarded accordingly: '. . . unethical conduct is shaped and conditioned by cultural attitudes and patterns of behaviour deeply rooted and profoundly institutionalised in the hearts and minds of both public servants and their clients. Therefore, attempts to reform public bureaucracies as independent systems are necessary but not sufficient' (Jabbra and Jabbra 1983: 140).

However, we are concerned with the ethical dimension of organizations from a number of different perspectives including the relationship between the organization and wider society, the purposes for which organizations are constituted and how they treat their staff in seeking to achieve those purposes. As Fukuyama (1995) and Arrow (1974) argue, private sector organizations and market relations are underpinned by an ethical bedrock. It is, however, a legitimate question to ask if the purposes of private sector organizations have moral purposes in the same way that public services do. This is a key issue in business ethics. Sternberg (1994), for example, argues that what constitutes ethical conduct in business depends on a business's definitive purpose which she defines as maximizing long-term owner value through selling goods and services. A business may do other things but this is its core activity and using business resources for non-business purposes constitutes, according to Sternberg, theft. She argues that: 'An organisation which pursued moral goodness simply because it was good, would simply be not acting as a business' (p. 96).

Sternberg (1994) does support the benefits of distributive justice to employees on the basis of contribution to owner value. As we have seen, it can be argued that business depends upon government for infrastructure and that business cannot exist in isolation from the community. Even markets are regulated. Hosmer (1994) builds his arguments concerning ethical business on a number of propositions which hypothesize that companies operating in a competitive global economy are dependent upon a wide range of stakeholders for cooperative activities and that it is possible to build trust, commitment and effort on the part of all stakeholders by including ethical principles in the strategic decision-making of companies where the interests and rights of all stakeholders are recognized.

However, perhaps a more convincing argument for the ethical private sector organization can be made on the basis of how it treats its staff rather than what its purposes are, and the issues raised here will apply to any organization. Golembiewski (1992), revisiting an article that he published originally in 1962, describes a number of values which should exist in organizations and what impact they may have on high performance:

- Work must be psychologically acceptable and non-threatening. This will be compatible with both personality and job requirements.
- Work must allow employees to develop their skills through job enlargement and job training.
- The task must allow the individual room for self-determination and self-development.
- Workers must be encouraged to influence the environment within which they work through group decision-making, peer representation in promotion, self-choice of work unit members and decentralization.
- The formal organization must not be the sole and final arbiter of behaviour; decentralization and group decision-making will play a part.

Golembiewski (1992) believes that organizations should be driven by ethical considerations and be compatible with the Judaeo-Christian set of values. Whether any organizations act in such a way is a moot point. Golembiewski's arguments are normative rather than based upon evidence. However, returning to our discussion of public services organizations we can pose the following questions:

- What social good do they perform?
- How do they distribute their resources among those from whom they derive their legitimacy?
- How do we distinguish between private interests and the public good?
- How do public service organizations treat their staff?
- How do different stakeholders view the role of public services organizations?

Galbraith (1993: 71) makes the point that in the first instance we have to distinguish between different types of public services organization: 'It will be evident . . . that those agencies and departments that serve contentment have a standing in public attitude and expression very different from those that collect taxes, succour the poor or enforce regulations'. According to this argument, we have an adverse attitude towards welfare bureaucracy but a positive attitude towards the military!

The purposes of public services organizations are diverse and may, indeed, be in conflict. Prison service agencies are generally expected to extract retribution while delivering rehabilitation. Not only that but there will be different types of goals. Mintzberg (1983) distinguishes between system goals and mission goals. Some organizations are strong on mission goals: 'Our aim is to transform the well-being of the local community'. Others might be characterized by system goals such as acting in an economic and efficient manner in the collection of taxes.

At one level, organizations have purposes and we might judge them from a consequentialist approach; do they do more good than harm? At another level, they are places where individuals engage with each other for a good deal of their lives, and we might judge them from a deontological perspective; do they encourage employees to treat each other with respect and dignity and not use each other as a means to an end? Reiser (1994: 28) argues: 'Yet organizations declare what really counts by their treatment of staff, the institutional goals they set, and how they handle controversy and conflicts. What they do tells us what they value'. Reiser argues that healthcare organizations are made up of different stakeholders and these must be brought together to constitute the ethical fabric of the organization. Relationships and responsibilites will reflect a concern with values and be linked to goals. Reiser argues that as healthcare organizations have taken on more non-medical staff there has been a shift in authority from the medical profession to marketing, financial and management specialists. This has led to rivalry which is exacerbated by the fact that different stakeholders will have different training and sets of values. This is also the case in university business schools with a proliferation of marketing staff and administrative backup concerned with evaluation, for example. Their commitment may be to get the students through the door irrespective of what goes on in teaching or whether the course offered is the most suitable.

The organization will have relationships with outside bodies. A healthcare institution may believe that it also has a commitment to future generations as part of the community and believe that it has a duty to preserve resources for future patients. This is all about the organization recognizing who its stakeholders are, both present and future. There are ethical responsibilities through sharing a common geographical area; organizations are rooted in the community they serve. These responsibilities are best met by internal stakeholders working in a cooperative relationship to serve the benefits of the community. Yet there may be disagreements about what the best interests of the community are, who defines them and how they are to be achieved. We need to separate what an organization does from what we think it should do.

An organization is an historical entity. It was created to serve a set of goals: 'The traditions of an organization set it apart from the individuals who work in and direct it. The accumulation of traditions as ways of doing things constructs the identity of the organization' (Reiser 1994: 32). We need to understand how organizations work before we can address the issues of how individuals operate within them.

Organizational forms and structures

Classical bureaucracies were organized along hierarchical lines to ensure the advantages of specialization, accountability and management control, centralization and the allocation of clear tasks and responsibilities. However, as we discussed above, public services organizations perform different functions and perform different goals, and structures will reflect this. The link between structure and goals can be put very simply: structure should reflect goals. If our public services are expected to be innovative, responsive to the environment and deliver flexible services it would not make sense to have a rigid, inflexible, hierarchical organization bound by rules.

The Local Government Management Board (1993) identified the different functions that local authorities can perform:

1 Direct service provision. This function characterized the old-style councils, involving professional dominance, hierarchical management with central control, individuals seen as clients rather than customers and a paternalistic attitude to clients. We may wonder at the extent to which this type of organization still exists.
2 The commercial approach. This approach is adopted by the type of local authority which is characterized by client-contractor splits, is driven by commercial not professional considerations, uses contracts and makes extensive use of outside contractors. Its main role is to monitor contractors and it therefore needs a system for performance evaluation and review. There is a belief in private sector practices and there is a slimmed-down workforce.
3 Community governance. The authority that adopts this function focuses on the community and civic leadership; it is characterized by cross-departmental strategies to combat poverty, for example. It adopts a corporate style, has an outward-looking external orientation and promotes the area to outsiders.
4 The neighbourhood approach. This approach involves the use of area committees and supports participatory democracy, with a strong role for back-benchers. It is area rather than function based. The authority is involved in partnerships with the voluntary sector and is concerned with access, participation, devolved management and a close relationship with users.

You will recall that in our examination of the public service ethos in Chapter 4, Pratchett and Wingfield (1994) found that different types of authority perceived the public service ethos in different ways. However, different purposes mean that the public interest will be defined in different places, perhaps in the community, the neighbourhood or with customers.

There will be different sets of relationships, from a direct provider role to a contractor role.

In what ways does the bureaucratic form of organization affect individuals? It is often assumed that bureaucracies are pathological and dysfunctional for the individuals who work in them and have the directly opposite effect than the one described by Golembiewski (1992) in the previous section. It is argued that any organization that is characterized by a rational organization of social interaction may be fundamentally incapable of taking care of goals and policies that require human interaction (Hummel 1987). One phrase from Weber (1968), in *Economy and Society*, has done more than anything to support this view: 'Bureaucracy develops the more perfectly it is "dehumanized"' (p. 975).

The dysfunctions of bureaucracy are said to include:

- Individuals in bureaucracies become conservative and resist change.
- Bureaucrats become dependent upon external sanctions for motivation.
- Bureaucracy focuses on meritocracy and does not promote teamwork.
- Leaders lead and others follow.
- Bureaucrats are not willing to give up power.
- Bureaucracy encourages group think where existing norms remain unchallenged.
- Bureaucracy fosters mistrust and fear.
- Bureaucracy stresses the formal rather than the informal organization.
- Bureaucracy encourages excessive rule-following.
- Bureaucrats can hide behind rules, as an excuse for not using judgement.
- Bureaucrats are expected to conform to certain role expectations.
- Bureaucrats are expected to 'keep their noses clean' and not violate role norms.
- There is strong personal loyalty to superiors.

We may not agree that all of these are dysfunctional. Depending upon the context, personal loyalty to superiors might be considerd a virtue rather than being dysfunctional. However, critics argue that in normal life people relate to each other through the meaning each attaches to his or her action. The bureaucrat, on the other hand, is restricted to those actions permitted by the job rules and programme requirements. According to Hummel (1987), organizational relationships are different from social relationships which usually consist of two discrete individuals, each capable of putting themselves in the other's shoes, and who have a common perception of a shared world.

What are the characeristics of bureaucratic relationships? According to Hummel (1987):

- Bureaucracies consist of an individual, the manager, and a 'pseudo-being', the functionary.

- The manager treats the functionary as a means rather than an end.
- Both lack a common perception of a shared reality and both are prohibited from reciprocal interaction for constructing a shared reality, the manager retaining a monopoly on defining organizational reality.
- The manager speaks a language to the functionary that is totally instructional and one-directional and does not allow for any mutual redefinition of the relationship.

However, in a polemic in support of bureaucracy, Goodsell (1994) examines the notion that bureaucracy is said to treat human beings callously, that it is oppressive both to its clients and its employees. He considers the arguments that bureaucrats are passive agents of the institution, that specialism leads to narrowness, that it is unfulfilling and dehumanizing. According to the rhetoric this is linked to the way in which the organization treats its clients. Bureaucrats treat individuals as impersonal objects, as cases, controlled and restricted. Operational discretion also gives scope for racial and other forms of discrimination to be condoned. What is the evidence for this? Certainly, as far as the outputs of bureaucracy are concerned, Goodsell argues that both individual citizen surveys and national surveys all point to the same conclusion: 'Most citizens are satisfied with their personal experiences with bureaucracy most of the time' (p. 29). This argument is supported by the recent survey in the UK by the Public Management Foundation (1997) involving 1000 individuals in four different geographical areas. Satisfaction levels with local performance in education, health and policing were high. Education scored a 73 per cent satisfaction rate, health 72 per cent and policing 56 per cent. These services seem to be performing rather better than critics would have us believe. The consistent message in all three services was that there should be much greater involvement of local people in setting performance indicators and that local managers should be given more power. Politicians, particularly at central level should be kept well away! What are we to conclude from this? The provision of public services appears to be well received by their users, and it is the normative view of politicians that appears to be a problem. The perception of bureaucracy held by different stakeholders is very different. But are these high satisfaction levels on the part of citizens mirrored if we ask employees? This is the other part of the equation.

Goodsell (1994, see Chapter 4) argues that there are four ways in which bureaucracy is programmed to fail:

1 It is charged with achieving inconsistent, contradictory and hence unachievable goals and tasks.
2 Its capacities are undermined by its having to achieve results indirectly through the efforts of others.
3 We measure bureaucracy not by how much it tries to move ahead on an impossible front but whether or not 'success' is achieved.

4 The role of bureaucracy in achieving social change is misrepresented in that we both oversell and undersell what it can achieve.

The bureaucrat's task is inherenty difficult since:

- there is often an antisocial or non-cooperative client;
- they are often dealing with controversial issues in areas of public policy where there is considerable disagreement; e.g. dealing with unemployment;
- there is the absence of a prestigious profession; e.g. as in social work;
- there is often popular non-acceptance of the mission; e.g. as in tax collection.

Reporting on the evidence, Goodsell argues that bureaucrats are pretty much like everybody else. It is not the case that perfectly ordinary human beings suddenly become petty tyrants when they go through the office door unless either the organization transforms them or the work transforms them, perhaps through dealing with certain claimants or criminals. Goodsell concludes:

> We discover . . . that the empirical evidence reviewed to verify the 'bureaucratic mentality' does very little to assure us that it actually exists. Bureaucrats have not been shown to be less flexible and open-minded than nonbureaucrats, and they do not appear more rule oriented. Indeed, much evidence points to little difference between bureaucrats and ordinary people . . . With respect to attitudes towards clients, welfare bureaucrats, despite their reputation for being disrespectful and overzealous rule enforcers, tend to perceive clients as honest and deserving. They even seem quite sympathetic to them and are prepared to bend the rules in their favor.
>
> (1994: 123)

In fact, theorists do distinguish between different types of bureaucrat. Downs (1967: 92–111) identified five bureaucratic personality types:

1 Climbers who want to maximize their own power, prestige and income.
2 Conservers who are equally egotistic, but want a quiet life and a stable future.
3 Zealots who constitute a mixed type.
4 Advocates who have a more general idealistic orientation.
5 Statesmen who take a broader view of the general welfare. These approximate to the model of the altruistic civil servant.

Public choice theory is based on the premise that officials are budget maximizers and act rationally in seeking to increase their budgets. Dunleavy (1991) tries to reconstruct the public choice model from the perspective of bureau-shaping rather than budget maximizing which takes account of other utility considerations for senior officials such as those that are work-related rather than purely financial. He also links the model to different types of agencies such as:

- delivery agencies (which conform to classical bureaucracy);
- regulatory agencies;
- transfer agencies (benefits or pensions);
- contracts agencies;
- control agencies;
- taxing agencies;
- trading agencies;
- servicing agencies.

The list demonstrates the diversity of public services agencies. Yet Self (1977: 4) recognized that: 'The Weberian model of a hierarchical, rule-dominated administration still has some validity for some parts of the system but not for others. Public administration has become a patchwork quilt of complex relationships and numerous decision points, on which new forms of politics are brought to bear'.

The fabric of the organization

As we saw earlier, organizations are historical entities comprising values and are enshrined in a tradition. Values, traditions and culture can be illustrated by the use of the term 'organizational fabric'. Oakeshott's concept of a tradition is described as follows:

> Now a tradition of behaviour is a tricky thing to get to know indeed, it may even appear to be essentially unintelligible. It is neither fixed nor finished, it has no changeless centre to which understanding can anchor itself; there is no sovereign purpose to be perceived or invariable direction to be detected, there is no model to be copied, idea to be realised, or rule to be followed. Some parts of it may change more slowly than others, but none is immune from change. Everything is temporary. Nevertheless though a tradition of behaviour is flimsy and elusive, it is not without identity, and what makes it a possible object of knowledge is the fact that all its parts do not change at the same time and that the changes it undergoes are potential within it. Its principle is a principle of continuity; authority is diffused between past, present, and future: between the old, the new and what is to come. It is steady because, though it moves, it is never wholly in motion: and though it is tranquil it is never wholly at rest.
>
> (1962: 128)

This lengthy quote captures the nature of public services organizations which are often full of ambiguity, diversity and intangible ways of working.

According to Bridges (1950: 16):

> . . . in every Department [there is] a store of knowledge and experi-
> ence in the subjects handled, something which eventually takes shape
> as a practical philosophy, or may merit the title of a departmental
> philosophy . . . in most cases the departmental philosophy is nothing
> more startling than the slow accretion an accumulation of experience
> over the years . . . Every civil servant finds himself [*sic*] entrusted with
> this kind of inheritance. He knows that it is his business to contribute
> something of his own to this store of experience; and that he should
> play his part in moulding it and improving it to meet changing condi-
> tions. Equally he knows that it is something he will ignore at his peril.

Problems arise if that philosophy becomes ossified; if the traditions act as
a barrier to change. The power of these traditions needs to be recognized
by those who seek to bring about organizational change.

As previously discussed, Heclo and Wildavsky (1981) use the concept of
the village to describe relations within the Treasury which is populated by
'kinsmen' speaking in a common idiom. The numbers involved are only a
few hundred and their relations with each other are characterized by mutual
trust. The work of the Treasury is passed on from one generation to the
next such that novices are inculcated in the Treasury way of doing things.
The 'Treasury view' is formed by informal conversations, the Treasury acts
as a coordinating mechanism and cooperation is fostered by the fact that
those at the top will have come across each other many times. The perspective is that of a club and this view is not new. Young and Sloman
(1984) uncovered this sense of intimacy where everybody appears to know
everybody else. They quote an undersecretary: 'Some of these people I've
known for twenty-five years and we can of course communicate with each
other almost in code' (p. 25). Hennessy (1990: 521) comments that: 'Their
habits, modes of thought, patterns of speech, style of drafting will have
rubbed off one to another to the point where but a few free or tough or
independent spirits resit mutation into a sludgy administrative amalgam'.

It is these traditions that lead to the assumption of a unified service
where officials adhere to a common ethos. In a similar fashion, Richards
(1996: 671–2) argues that:

> The British police service, with its long and creditable tradition, has
> evolved a body of practice, a way of going about things, which is
> generally responsive to the society which it serves. The individual
> police officer is initiated into this practice and learns much of the
> substance of his work through a process of apprenticeship in which
> good conduct is understood as appropriate participation in the act-
> ivities of policing. The rules, formal and informal, which guide his
> practice are generally assimilated into his outlook and help form his

actions. Many of these rules are not so much the product of design but the product of countless long-forgotten choices which encapsulate suggestions of how to achieve practical results. Others are those which relate to the prudential arts of the job: those which embody the hints, tips and clues which prescribe the sort of officer who is acceptable to his colleagues, of all ranks.

Traditions and practices are linked to human action. Thus there is a wealth of material concerning how individuals behave which is addressed fully in the social philosophy literature. One example is illustrated by a quote from one of the best-known books in this field:

> Human action cannot be properly identified, or understood, unless we take account of the intentional descriptions, the meanings that such actions have for the agents involved, and the ways in which they interpret their own actions and the actions of others. These intentional descriptions, meanings and interpretations are not merely subjective states of mind which can be correlated with external behaviour: they are constitutive of the activities and practices of our social and political lives.
>
> (Bernstein 1976: 229)

And we might add organizational lives. What is being said is that action is best understood in terms of a practice – it is that which gives it meaning and forms the 'social construction of reality'.

Organizational culture and control

In organizational theory the most common approach to understanding the informal workings of organizations has been through culture, defined by Schein (1987: 6) as: '. . . basic assumptions and beliefs that are shared by members of an organization, that operate unconsciously, and that define in a basic "taken-for-granted" fashion an organization's view of itself and its environment. These assumptions and beliefs are learned responses to a group's problems of survival in its external environment and its problems of internal integration'. Culture is not the same as values or corporate philosophy, but underpins them. It is concerned with people, with basic goals and functions. It is reinforced by structure, systems and procedures, design of physical space, stories, myths and legends, important events and people, and formal statements of the organization's philosophy and creed.

We seem to be working with a family of concepts that describe the way in which 'we do things around here' and what this means for us. These concepts include traditions, culture and ethos, philosophy and values. According to Schein (1987: 128–34) organizational culture will be expressed in five different dimensions:

1 The organization's relationship with its environment: what does the organization stand for and how does it relate to the outside world; through a community or a contractual approach?
2 The organization's basic assumptions about reality and decisions, including issues concerning traditions and the way it makes decisions through, in the public services, politicians, senior managers, professionals and so on. The organization will also be concerned with basic issues concerning time and space. Is it oriented towards the past or the future? Does the civil service look back to some golden age of a 'Rolls Royce' service? How does it conceive of space; e.g. central-local relations perhaps?
3 The nature of human nature: what view does it take? Basically bad, good, or neutral?
4 The nature of human activity: is it responsive or reactive, innovative or inert?
5 The nature of human relations: is it collegial, individual, autocratic, or participative?

Subcultures

Cultural norms within an organization can socialize workers into rule following or rule breaking. Sinclair (1993) examines different approaches to organizational culture. One approach is that which sees culture in unitary terms built around an overt statement of organizational values. One task of senior management will be to reinforce values and to ensure conformity to those values on the part of employees. However, as Sinclair points out, such a strong commitment to creating an organizational culture is questionable if it involves coercion. Not only that but in the long term adherence to an existing culture may promote conservatism and rigidity and drive out innovation and diversity. A second approach to organizational culture recognizes the existence of subcultures where values and norms are located. The problems arise when one subculture holds to a different set of ethical principles. Sinclair argues that the subculture approach to ethics in organizations is one which can recognize diversity and cope with cultural relativism. The risk of the first approach is that organizational ethics are those of a managerial elite and are not internalized by the rest of the organization. The risk of the second approach is that subcultures may pull in different directions, leaving management unable to find a common strategy.

Van Maanen and Barley (1984: 294–5) discuss this organizational diversity in terms of occupational communities: 'By occupational community, we mean a group of people who consider themselves to be engaged in the same sort of work; who identify (more or less positively) with their work; who share a set of values, norms and perspectives that apply to, but extend beyond, work-related matters; and whose social relationships meld the realms of work and leisure'.

An occupational community consists of:

- Boundaries: usually set by members themselves. It is they who decide who is in and who is out.
- Social identity: members derive self-images from their occupational role. This also means that members communicate with each other in terms of a common language. This is reinforced by the feeling of being special.
- Reference groups: to maintain a social identity, support and confirmation from others is necessary. This will include such issues as what is to count as 'good' or 'bad' conduct. Thus there are no relevant ethical universal standards to be measured against, but there is peer evaluation.
- Social relations: this is the blurring of the distinction between work and leisure. People live and work together. We can often see this in those communities which spring up around a particular industry or company.

Self-control of occupational matters is a key consideration for occupational groups. The occupational community stretches beyond the workplace. Self-control can be threatened by damaging public disclosures which reveal practices most members would like to keep private. Demystifying them is to undo them! Unionization and professionalization are means through which control over the workplace can be secured. Professionals are a distinct group because of the success they have had in claiming occupational self-control. Administrative concerns such as efficiency, quality control and specialization tend to increase in salience in bureaucracies and to drive out occupationally-based traditions and interests. From the caseworker's perspective, managerial demands for people processing and properly documenting the eligibility of clients eliminates any opportunity to really help people in need.

Managers will try to control occupational communties. Critics of managerialism argue that:

> The fact that managerialism is shrouded in the language of efficiency and public interests is a mere smokescreen. In the case of local government, managerialism is more about reshaping the organization into a control agency for the benefit of professional staff and to the detriment of lower skilled outdoor workers.
>
> Moving into the managerialism fold offers the senior manager the opportunity to reduce the number of blue-collar workers and expand the number of supervisory and professional situations, which increases his or her control and thereby improves the agency's status and character.
>
> (Albin 1995: 140)

However, we may wonder at the extent to which the evidence supports this view. In condemning the whole of senior management as control maximizers, the author may be falling into the same trap as those who advocate the virtues of management skills, particularly when assumed to be practised in the private sector. Critics of managerialism in Australia for example argue:

- Managers have experienced greater autonomy in decison-making but at the expense of professional autonomy.
- The new manager brings skills in personnel or financial management to the organization. It appears that there is no longer any requirement for substantial professional knowledge or experience. Nor do staff see that a commitment to clients is a prerequisite for managerial jobs.
- Clients and their needs are viewed as inputs and outcomes.
- 'When the new managers arrive to convert an old organisation to managerialist values and language they like to disown the past, as though nothing happened before they arrived or, if it did, nothing good could be said about it' (Rees 1995: 198).

As Gowler and Legge (1996: 42) argue: 'The rhetoric of bureacuractic control uses the language of accountability and accounting to help construct a "moral environment" where the hierarchical ordering of roles and relationships is equated with the responsible conduct of human affairs, and where the "right to manage" is extended to become "the right to manage power and exchange relationships"'.

Organizational control and individual morals

We are concerned with what the organization can legitimately demand of the individual. We are concerned with the rights and responsibilities of individuals towards the organization. The relationship has to be two-way or even three-way to include other stakeholders such as clients, citizens and customers. Organizations in both the public and private sectors have changed their configurations, their structures and the employer-employee relationship. Many organizations now have different kinds of employees on different kinds of contracts. Will Hutton (1996) has defined the 30:30:40 society which consists of the disadvantaged, the marginalized and insecure, and the privileged. Hutton argues that it is only the privileged 40 per cent who have some security in the job market. He argues that two-thirds of all new jobs offered to the unemployed are part-time or temporary. This will have an effect on the relationship between the organization and its employees. Will the same kind of commitment be generated among those on short-term contracts? What is the responsibility of the firm for the employment practices of sub-contractors? What kind of an association is the organization? The questionnaire presented in Box 6.1 is an example of how this might be established.

Box 6.1 Questionnaire

In your organization

	Always	Often	Sometimes	Never
1 Do people relate to and treat each other as a whole person or as a specialist to be consulted for their professional expertise?				
2 Is each member of the organization perceived as having equal worth?				
3 Are communications open and founded on trust?				
4 Are obligations mutual, diffuse and extended?				
5 Are relationships both within and outside the organization dominated by contracts?				
6 Is there a sense of belonging together and sharing a common identity?				
7 Are personal development, security and satisfaction perceived to be important?				
8 Are you encouraged to treat others and their ideas with respect?				
9 Is power maintained by keeping information from others?				
10 Does top management show a commitment to moral conduct?				
11 How keen is the organization to uncover and discipline immoral conduct when it occurs?				
12 Is internal criticism of policies and practices encouraged?				
13 Are people afraid to report immoral behaviour for fear of reprisals?				
14 Do staff not report instances of immoral behaviour because their co-workers would ostracize them?				
15 Do you feel that you have to compromise your ethical principles to conform to organizational expectations?				
16 Do you believe that performance pressure sometimes leads to immoral conduct?				

What is the basis for structuring organizational and interorganizational relationships? Is it:

- Autocracy: based on the view that leaders and owners have the power and the right and the duty to exercise it.
- Paternalism: based on the notion that those in power have an obligation to take care of those who are not.
- Consultation: all have something to contribute but power is with the leaders.
- Participation: power is shared where appropriate.
- Delegation: power is located where skill resides but accountability remains in managerial roles; managers must therefore trust their staff.
- Collegiality: partners who share full responsibility.

The following case study illustrates the impact of organizational power relations, and the resulting stress, on individuals.

Case study: Promotion and patronage in further education

From 1 April 1993 some 500 further education colleges in England and Wales were given corporate status, releasing them from local education authority (LEA) control. The rationale for the change was that self-government would encourage colleges to be more efficient, effective, flexible and entrepreneurial. Control of resources was now firmly with the senior management of the colleges. Over time the colleges introduced new contracts for staff and persuaded staff to move from the old LEA 'silver book' contracts. Most staff, in return for salary increases agreed to shorter holidays and more class contact time. A handful of staff chose to remain on the old contracts, foregoing any pay increases, for a number of reasons. One major reason was the feeling that quality was bound to go down if staff did not have time to prepare lessons and that students would receive a diluted educational experience as lecturers' class contact time increased. The senior management of some colleges resented the 'silver book' employees who were less flexible than those who had agreed to new contracts.

Sally had just been promoted head of business studies in a college of further education. She had previously been deputy head and the department also had an assistant head. Sally's old post was advertised internally and eight staff applied. Sally along with the head of personnel and the director of the college met to shortlist the candidates. At this meeting the head of personnel and the director announced that only three candidates would be shortlisted, irrespective of the quality of the candidates, and that as two of the candidates had already been promoted by them and Sally's predecessor in the past they had to be interviewed again. These two candidates were not rated by the rest of the staff. However, the head of personnel and the director felt that if these two had not been interviewed it would be tantamount to admitting past mistakes. One of them was the existing assistant head who assumed that the promotion was hers. The second candidate had been promoted to a coordinating role that had never materialized. A third candidate was also interviewed from another department and was subsequently given the job. This third candidate was very able and had been passed over for promotion a number of times. She had recently agreed to give up her 'silver book' contract and sign a new contract.

The appointment was a popular choice with the other staff in the department except that many expressed amazement that a fourth candidate, Anne, had not even been shortlisted. This candidate ran the biggest course in the school which was a franchise from the local university and was very high profile. Anne had, in her own time, studied for and passed an MBA and was more highly qualified than anyone else in the department. Anne's name was always the first to be put forward when any management courses were requested by local businesses. However, she had refused to sign a new contract because she believed in maintaining quality and had been threatened with dismissal. This, and her belief in personal development in areas that would benefit her teaching, were seen as signalling a lack of commitment to the college. Sally argued vociferously for her inclusion on the shortlist but in the end went along with the decision not to include Anne.

When the result came out Anne went to see Sally to find out why she had not been shortlisted. After an hour and a half of feedback which failed to provide a satisfactory answer, Sally finally admitted in confidence that 'it was all political and you have had a raw deal'. The two failed candidates also felt badly treated, particularly the existing assistant head who felt that her expectations had been raised.

All of this took place at the end of the summer term and resentment had fizzled out when the new term starts in September. However, Sally desperately tries to meet the targets set by senior managers and increases class sizes and reduces the hours of part-time lecturers. She also has to implement a senior management decision to reduce their hourly rate. Morale in the department begins to fall. Sally exhausts herself trying single-handedly to compensate for the perceived inadequacies of senior management and for the perceived injustices perpetrated by the organization. She realizes that staff have been unjustly treated and are suffering the consequences of irresponsible management. She takes it upon herself to rectify some of these injustices, suffers stress and 'burn-out' and leaves.

Sally is put in the invidious position of trying to reconcile her career with her conscience. She can do this in nine different ways:

1 Don't think about it; just go along and get along.
2 Protest and suffer the consequences.
3 Conscientiously object.
4 Leave.
5 If injustices are being perpetrated, secretly blow the whistle.
6 Publicly blow the whistle.
7 Secretly threaten to blow the whistle.
8 Sabotage.
9 Negotiate and build a consensus for the future.

The issue of the employees commitment to perform for the organization is a key one and has four main components:

1 The extent to which the individual has internalized the values of the organization which, in turn, will depend on how congruent individual and organizational values are.

2 The extent to which organizational objectives reflect individual objectives.
3 The extent of the involvement with and psychological immersion in work.
4 The extent to which individuals value the organization as a place to spend their lives.

As McKevitt and Lawton (1996: 53) argue in their study of performance management:

> The lack of attention paid to the need to gain commitment from middle management is symptomatic of a 'command and control' view of organizational dynamics. Senior managers and politicians decide on the desired direction of change and then proceed to implement a top-down process of change. Such a strategy ... does not reflect the organizational or cultural character of many public services.

This is not unique to the UK. In analysing the public sector management reforms in Canada, known as PS2000, Caiden *et al.* (1995: 97) argue that these reforms have a double edge to them: 'They have experienced greater responsibilities, authority and accountability, greater accompanying stress in implementing changes they often had no part in creating, and greater morale problems resulting from simultaneous pressures to produce higher quality services while having to retrench staff'.

The concept of reform is a very attractive one, while the actual implementation of reform reveals problems and drawbacks. How many organizations undergo restructuring because of a new director? Because it is new it must be good! There is often a human cost that is overlooked.

Whistleblowing

Whistleblowing is concerned with employees revealing information publicly which the organization does not want revealed to an outside party. It is not to be undertaken lightly since there is an implied duty of fidelity to the organization, such that employees should not act, in general, in ways that are contrary to their employer's interests. Yet there are 'just cause' defences. Whistleblowing is used to describe the act of raising a concern about a serious danger to the public, workplace, environmental health or safety, or some other serious misconduct or malpractice and the failure of the organization to act. It is the disclosure of confidential information in circumstances where an individual's own sense of morality and conscience, his or her duty of loyalty to the employer and indeed the wider public interest demands that the disclosure be made. If the disclosure is made and then ignored by the employer, with the result that a serious or fatal accident occurs, then the organization will be required to explain its failure to act. Whistleblowing is an essential part of the wider debate concerning accountability, good governance and organizational ethics. (See Public Concern at Work 1995.)

Whistleblowing may be justified according to the response to such questions as:

- Is the organization's action lawful or is it illegal?
- Is the action unconstitutional?
- Has the matter been raised internally?
- Has information been made public as a last resort?
- Do mechanisms exist for raising such concerns internally?
- What is the issue?
- Does the action go against accepted standards of morality?

It is often difficult to raise an issue because of the feared reaction of the manager, loyalty (don't dob on your mates'), a belief that the complaint would not be investigated, or a lack of confidence that the complaint would be taken seriously. However, whistleblowing might be considered just where the individual:

- is not acting in bad faith;
- has reasonable grounds for believing the information is accurate;
- is not making the disclosure primarily in order to make financial gain;
- raised the matter internally first.

Case studies: Whistleblowing

Case 1

Clive Ponting, a senior civil servant in the Ministry of Defence, leaked information to an opposition MP concerning the sinking of the Argentine ship *Belgrano* during the Falklands War. Ponting argued that government ministers had lied to Parliament and that it was in the public interest that this information should be made public. Ponting argued that he had a duty to Parliament and the public interest over and above that of the government of the day. Ponting was put on trial and acquitted.

Case 2

In 1983 Sarah Tisdall, a clerk working in the foreign secretary's office, leaked documents to the *Guardian* newspaper, documents written by the then defence secretary, Michael Heseltine concerned with the arrival of cruise missiles at Greenham Common air base. Tisdall believed that Heseltine was not going to be accountable to Parliament and she was also generally disenchanted with government policies. She was given six months imprisonment.

Again the issue is one of the location of duty; is it to Parliament rather than the government of the day? Who should loyalty be given to? Who is the employer? This is not always clear. In the USA the civil servant's first loyalty is to the public interest and not to the government of the day.

Case 3

In 1994 James Pain, an administrative officer in the Civil Service, was disciplined for complaining publicly about industrial tribunal rooms remaining empty while applicants wait one or two years for hearings. He disclosed official information without authorization. He wrote to the president of the industrial tribunals with copies to the prime minister, the lord chancellor, the leader of the opposition and the *Guardian* newspaper.

Case 4

Westminster City Council has been at the centre of a major scandal. The council was found guilty of gerrymandering wards at the expense of suspected Labour-voting homeless people to ensure that the council remained Conservative in 1987. The district auditor undertook an eight-year investigation. The council appealed to the Nolan Inquiry to introduce penal powers to prosecute councillors and officials who leak confidential information which could expose corruption. The former leader Dame Shirley Porter with five other councillors and officers were facing a £31 million surcharge at the time of writing!

However, those who do blow the whistle may still have to work in an organization afterwards. There are practical considerations involved. A report in the *Guardian* newspaper on 28 July 1988, entitled 'Whistleblowers saved from a US gulag' (Erlichman 1988) based on 233 American whistleblowers found that:

- 90 per cent lost their jobs or were demoted;
- 27 per cent faced lawsuits;
- 26 per cent faced psychiatric and medical referral;
- 25 per cent admitted to alcohol abuse;
- 17 per cent lost their homes;
- 15 per cent divorced during the aftermath;
- 10 per cent attempted suicide;
- 8 per cent went bankrupt.

Now whether these figures would constitute a cross-section of any population is a moot point and whether whistleblowing was the cause of these individuals' misfortunes is not made clear, but it still makes sorry reading. The implication is that it was down to the act of whistleblowing and the strain that it puts on individuals. Whistleblowers are seen as highly moral people who are dismissed as loose cannons by their organization.

Conclusion

Organizations are constituted by fibres made up of traditions, cultures and practices. Although they do change over time, depending on how well they are embedded in the organizational fabric, immoral conduct can become institutionalized. Where this is the case, such conduct becomes difficult to change. At the same time, organizations do put pressure on individuals but only through other individuals. What would have happened in our case study involving promotion in the college if Sally had stood up to senior management and said 'What you are asking me to do is wrong and I will not do it. I will resign or you can take me off the interview panel'? How realistic a response is this? We turn to this issue in Chapter 9.

seven

Ethics and evaluation

Key issues

- In what ways does evaluation have an ethical dimension?
- To what extent is evaluation used as a system of managerial control?
- Should an ethical evaluation focus upon outcomes or processes?

Introduction

Evaluating the performance of any organization is crucial; no one could doubt that individuals have to be held to account for the way in which public funds are spent and we have to have some way of ensuring that objectives are being met. Problems arise when: objectives are translated into easily measured targets plucked out of thin air and then imposed on managers; or when targets are used as political tools to lambast the opposition; or when meeting targets becomes the overriding consideration of the organization at the expense of everything else; or when objectives are not clear or in conflict; or when objectives are qualitative in nature and do not lend themselves easily to measurement.

In many ways we live in the evaluative state; in education, health, the police service, local or central government, managers and professionals have had their work subject to inspections and compared to other organizations through league tables. Reports from the Audit Commission on, for example, child protection, spending on secondary schools, the average time taken to relet dwellings or the percentage of local authority expenditure funded by central government grants appear on a regular basis in the press. These were all reported in the *Guardian* newspaper on 21 March 1996 in an article headed 'Council tables give parties chance to score points'. The article compares the performance of Labour-led councils with Conservative-led councils. But is the evaluation of organizational performance just a political football to be kicked around by whoever wants to score goals against the opposition by arguing that the performance of a local authority or an NHS hospital has declined or improved depending upon which party is in power? Undeniably, political evaluation is a key consideration in the performance of public bodies.

Evaluation of government activities originally developed as a means of judging the success or otherwise of particular programmes. Although the evaluation of public policy programmes is nothing new, the methods used and the bodies charged with the task often are. The UK government is littered with the debris of techniques, committees and working parties that have sought to evaluate public policies. The Fulton Report (Fulton 1968) on the UK Civil Service argued that the work of government could be enhanced through improving management performance and clarifying objectives, a theme that was to be given impetus in subsequent years. In a package of reforms for the policy process in government the then prime minister, Edward Heath, introduced programme analysis and review (PAR), which was designed to ask fundamental questions concerning the continuing need for the provision of particular services. PAR later fell into disuse as support for it in government declined. This illustrates a key feature of such attempts to evaluate the work of government: support from key stakeholders such as ministers or senior officials is probably more important for their continued use than the quality of the techniques used or the logic of their findings.

Throughout the 1980s in the UK, central government departments underwent various reforms to improve the efficiency and effectiveness of government. The Rayner scrutinies, a series of reforms named after Sir Derek Rayner (brought in by Prime Minister Thatcher from Marks & Spencer), were conducted in government, designed to eliminate waste and inefficiency. The key concepts that characterized this period were economy, efficiency and effectiveness (the '3 Es'). Critics argued that the most prominent 'E' tended to be economy as cost-cutting appeared to be the main objective. Critics also argued that other 'E' factors could be used to evaluate government programmes including ethics, equity and environmental friendliness. Cynics argued that the most important 'E' of all was electability (Metcalfe and Richards 1990 provide a good account of 'Raynerism' and the efficiency strategy in central government). However, progress in improving performance in government had been slow and the *Next Steps* Cabinet Office report (Efficiency Unit 1988: 7) recommended that:

First: The work of each department must be organised in a way which focuses on the job to be done; the systems and structures must enhance the effective delivery of policies and services.

Second: The management of each department must ensure that their staff have the relevant experience and skills needed to do the tasks that are essential to effective government.

Third: There must be a real and sustained pressure on and within each department for continuous improvement in the value for money obtained in the delivery of policies and services (bold as original).

This is the report that led to the creation of agencies to deliver government programmes and policies. What is interesting about the recommendations is the recognition that objectives, systems, structures, people and skills are all important in improving performance.

In many ways, these developments have led to the 'performance culture' that has come to dominate public services in the UK and elsewhere. In Australia, New Zealand and a host of other OECD countries, federal and state governments have reformed their public services to concentrate on outcomes, targets and performance measures (see, for example, Hood 1996). Governments are now interested in such questions as 'What are the aims and objectives of this Agency? Why does it exist and what is it intended to achieve?' The focus on objectives, it is argued, allows responsibilities to be made explicit, provides evidence of success or failure, assists in staff motivation, provides a basis for planning, monitoring and review and enhances accountability.

However, the adoption of a performance culture has had unintended consequences, as reported in the *Guardian* newspaper on 16 April 1997: 'Fake job figures scandal exposed'. According to this report hundreds of thousands of jobs found for the unemployed by the government's Employment Service were in fact created by 'fiddled figures, phantom placement scams and double counting . . .'. This resulted from pressure to hit targets. The article quoted Paul Convey, director of the Unemployment Unit pressure group, who described the scams as '. . . target culture gone mad. Jobcentres are being forced to put their efforts into creating imaginary figures to hit their targets rather than helping the unemployed back into work'.

Although the growth of government, with the creation of the welfare state, was an important impetus to the use of performance and evaluation methods, that use was based upon the assumption that government is concerned with improving social conditions. This view has not gone unchallenged and a prominent theme of the 1980s and 1990s has been to question whether government should be providing certain services at all. The challenge of the New Right has been that the private sector may deliver government services better, although what is to count as 'better' is open to question. A key distinction can be made, however, between 'doing things right' and 'doing the right thing'. Doing things right may involve a concern with economy, efficiency and so on; it may be a technical matter of finding the appropriate criteria to measure. Doing the right thing is a different kind of activity. In an article on performance indicators in the public services, Kanter and Summers (1987) use the phrase 'doing well while doing good' which captures the normative dimension to evaluation in the public services. If we distinguish between outputs and outcomes, a key consideration for the public services is whether it was worth carrying out a policy or programme in the first place i.e. is its impact likely to be of benefit to citizens?

The ethical context

In the public sector one of the most fundamental objectives of evaluation is to ensure the accountability of the organization (the agent) to its principals. One problem is the possible number of stakeholders. Another problem is identifying the location of accountability and responsibility. Critics frequently comment that government ministers seem reluctant to admit responsibility for any activity that falls within their remit. Witness the continuing public feud between the former home secretary, Michael Howard, and the former head of the Prison Service Agency, Derek Lewis. After three inmates escaped from Parkhurst Prison in 1995 Lewis was sacked by Howard who argued that operational matters were clearly the responsibility of the chief executive of the Agency. In the same way, the growth in the number of quangos begs the question of the accountability of non-elected public bodies that are spending public funds (see Weir and Hall 1994).

Thompson (1980) argues that, because many different officials contribute in many different ways to the performance of government, it is very difficult to locate moral responsibility. He calls this the 'problem of many hands'. He argues that the classical model of politicians proposing and officials disposing has long been discredited. Of course, as we discussed when we examined bureaucracy, officials may choose to hide behind rules and regulations and the fact that they may argue that they are 'merely' carrying out orders cannot be sustained, as the use of discretion by managers is long-recognized. The 'freedom to manage' also implies the duty to take responsibility. Thompson argues that:

> Ascribing responsibility to officials as persons rather than simply as occupants of certain offices or as members of a collectivity relies on two criteria of moral responsibility. An official is morally responsible for an outcome insofar as (1) the official's actions or omissions are a cause of the outcome; and (2) these actions or omissions are not done in ignorance or under compulsion.
>
> (1980: 908)

It is wrong to make somebody responsible but not to give them authority; who owns the performance is a crucial question here. The shifting of responsibility, from the political to the managerial, as highlighted by the sacking of Derek Lewis, undermines notions of ministerial responsibility.

However, we discussed a number of ethical frameworks in Chapter 3 which can be used to make judgements concerning behaviour. Such frameworks can first offer us guidance in deciding how to act. Second, they provide an evaluation or a reason for judgement of that act. For example, we can use utilitarianism to evaluate a particular act – did it help more people than it harmed? The notion of evaluation from a number of stakeholder perspectives is important; who is doing the evaluation and why and what citeria are being used are crucial issues and entail ethical considerations. It is the case that no evaluation and no evaluator is value free. Often this is hidden behind the cloak of professionalism. For some, value for money is a plausible criterion but it is not the only criterion. Other criteria could include:

- Does it do more harm than good?
- Were rights protected, responsibilities taken, obligations fulfilled?
- Was accountability assured?
- Was consent given?
- Was individual autonomy protected?
- Was quality maintained?
- Was efficient and effective use made of public funds?
- Was waste avoided?

There are different criteria that could be used to evaluate performance. It is not just about measuring outcomes but about the actions to produce those outcomes i.e. a combination of means and ends. As we see in Box 7.1, the notion of good performance is contested.

Box 7.1 Defining good policing

Traditionally, good policing has been defined in terms of adherence to law such that any deviation from law and procedure is perceived to be poor policing. Discretion in the use of the law is not sanctioned. However, as we know, there are often competing organizational goals, different practices in different police services, different expectations from the community and so on. The exercise of discretion is inevitable. Norris and Norris (1993) argue that there are different approaches to evaluating the performance of the individual police officer.

The objectives approach
This view argues that good policing depends on the achievement of objectives or agreed goals. Policing by objectives assumes that there is agreement on objectives and that it is possible to measure their achievement. How do we measure police

performance? Is it in terms of clear-up rates? These depend on public reporting practices. Local police chiefs may have different local operational priorities: even defining the stakeholders can be a problem. Her Majesty's Inspectorate of Constabulary's definition of customers includes victims, suspects, callers, participative users and other users (the vast majority of the population).

The professional ethics approach

A code of professional ethics offers a guide to the conduct of police officers such that the duty of a police officer may be 'to act in the public interest', howsoever defined. Such codes are ultimately grounded in values and reflect the views of those who draw them up. Such codes are often unenforceable and are so general that they offer little in the way of guidance. Other value systems may also exist which cut across formal codes of conduct.

The generic competency approach

Generic competencies are defined and attempts are made to distinguish effective from ineffective performance. Special skills, abilities and characteristics are defined. The problem is to define effective performance from the perspectives of the different stakeholders. Will the client have the same view as the chief constable?

The interactionist approach

From this perspective 'good policing' is that which conforms to the values and norms of the occupational culture. According to Norris and Norris (1993) an ethnographic approach considers competence to arise from the actual practice of police officers rather than that which is in line with explicit organizational goals or values. From the ethnographic perspective, good policing is dependent upon the situation and it will be defined, partly, by the audience judging it. The nature of good policing, therefore, will be essentially contested. According to Norris and Norris, good practice must acknowledge the situational, organizational and wider social aspects of policing and the interrelationships between these three dimensions. They conclude by arguing that:

> Because police practice cannot be fully determined in advance by prescriptive policies or training manuals we would argue that there can be no ideal practice. Good practice cannot be simply taught or replicated but it can be developed. This development is a personal achievement that in part depends on the repeated application of skills and situated judgement. But it also depends on a morally informed professional self-awareness, which is most likely to be fostered by a critical community of practitioners.
>
> (1993: 219)

Evaluation is usually seen in terms of a calculation: the utilitarian approach. Does traditional performance measurement examine outcomes (teleology) and how can quality and processes, or means, be measured (deontology)? What is evaluation for? Is it about control and judgement or is it about development? Is it about hitting or missing targets or is it about becoming more ethical in some sense? Can we use the same criteria to evaluate the organization and individuals within it? These are legitimate questions to ask.

Models of performance measurement

What should we evaluate? A local authority performs a number of different roles: it is simultaneously a legal entity, a representative body, an organization that provides goods and services, a place where people work, an organization with a history, and a local body. It performs multiple functions. Organizations may comprise a range of diverse, overlapping and potentially contradictory activities. Organizations are not rational bodies. This is reflected in the difficulty of measuring performance: an architect working for a local authority may want to design public housing that pushes back the frontiers of architecture and wins design council awards; the local authority might be interested in affordable, secure, warm and hygienic housing in a pleasant environemnt. The different interests may not coincide. Colebatch (1995: 161) argues that:

> The form that evaluation takes reflects the understanding of the organ-
> ization on which it rests. To the extent that the organization is seen
> as coherent, instrumental and hierarchical, program evaluation is likely
> to focus on output and to strengthen central control. To the extent
> that the organization is seen as complex, multi-faceted and interact-
> ive, program evaluation is likely to focus on process and to facilitate
> negotiation amongst stakeholders.

Kanter and Summers (1987) argue that a multiple constituency approach is required when measuring performance to reflect the values and interests of multiple stakeholders:

- Institutional functions revolve around legitimacy renewal and resource attraction. These are concerned with the extent to which the organization can satisfy the external stakeholders that the organization relies on for its funds and its existence. For UK public services managers, this means satisfying the objectives of politicians and focuses on the organization and its political environment.
- Managerial functions focus on the internal stakeholders of an organization and the need to consider different interests, departmental or professional, when allocating resources.
- Technical functions are concerned with the effectiveness of the organization in providing its services. The key stakeholders here will be customers or clients.

There appears to be a measure of agreement on the technical dimension to performance indicators. The OECD (1994: 41–2) identifies the following as examples of good practice:

- Indicators should be consistent over time and among units.
- Comparison should only be made on a like-with-like basis.
- Measures and indicators should be simple, well-defined and easily understood and reflect all aspects which are important to decision-making.
- Indicators should as far as possible not be affected by external factors unrelated to performance and should not have dysfunctional consequences.
- Emphasis should be given to a limited number of key measures or indicators likely to give the biggest pay-off.
- Managers' performance appraisal should only be for those areas over which they have control.

A number of difficulties are also recognized:

- Defining the objectives of work of a complex nature, particularly when there are likely to be multiple or conflicting objectives.
- Lack of relevant and measurable targets for final output, quality and effectiveness.
- Lack of correlation of overall objectives with specific objectives and targets thus greatly diminishing their value.
- The relative inexperience of officials in the development and use of performance measures.
- Lack of capabilities of staff traditionally trained in financial evaluation.
- Lack of interest by political users and top-level managers.
- Lack of resources for building up the necessary information systems.
- Resistance to time-recording from staff and unions.
- The cost of performance measurement.
- The complexity involved in comprehending and integrating a large number of data sources quickly and effectively.

Similarly, Mayston (1985) identifies nine roles for performance indicators in the public services. Indicators should:

1 clarify objectives;
2 evaluate outcomes;
3 provide an input into managerial incentive schemes;
4 allow consumers to make informed choices;
5 indicate standards to be met by contractors;
6 indicate the effectiveness and contribution of different activities to overall policy;
7 act as triggers for remedial action;
8 assist in determining cost-effectiveness;
9 indicate areas of potential cost-saving.

The problem with this and similar approaches is that performance indicators tend to be seen as neutral reporting devices and very little attention is given to the organizational context within which they will be used. Not only that but it also tends to be assumed that the organizational objectives are unproblematic. We need to distingush between effective performance management and performance measurement. The former is not just a technical exercise. Box 7.2 illustrates how one public service defines performance management.

Box 7.2 The distinctive characteristics of effective performance management for the Australian public service

- Managers provide leadership and integrate performance management with other aspects of their work in managing people.
- People understand that their performance directly contributes to the ongoing success and viability of the agency.
- Individual and team responsibilities and their performance are clearly linked to the achievement of programme and corporate goals and the needs of clients.
- Individuals and teams have a clear understanding of their work responsibilities and the standards of work expected of them.
- Individuals and teams meet the standards of behaviour expected of public officials.
- Managers monitor and assess the performance of their people.
- Individuals and teams receive regular feedback on their performance against programme and corporate goals.
- Managers make use of the potential of all their people and develop their skills encouraging individual career planning.
- Improved and valued performance is recognized and rewarded.
- Managers seek to improve poor performance.

What is the key focus of the performance management system outlined in Box 7.2? It concentrates on what but not how. Public services have to focus on how performance is achieved as well as what is achieved. How we are treated by public bureaucracies matters and this is why most standards of performance for public officials will be concerned with conduct. The Australian public service has three main principles which underpin standards of conduct:

1 An officer should perform his or her duties with professionalism and integrity and efficiently serve the government of the day.
2 Fairness and equity are to be observed in official dealings with colleagues and members of the public.
3 Real or apparent conflicts of interest are to be avoided.

Officials are expected to: perform official duties with skill, care, and diligence using authority in an unbiased way; provide service and advice on entitlements in a professional manner to the public; treat colleagues and members of public with courtesy and sensitivity to their rights, aspirations and duties; and behave, at all times, in a manner which will enhance the reputation of the Australian public service.

Performance appraisal

Pollitt (1987) identifies three models for performance appraisal:

1 The managerial model: the aim of this model is to aid decisions about the deployment of staff and where appraisal centres on a reward and punishment system based upon managerial control and judgement.
2 The professional development model: the aim of this model is to raise professional standards, disseminate knowledge about good practice and improve communications between colleagues working in the same field or institution. It is linked to personal development.
3 The consumer model: the aim of this model is to increase the responsiveness of the providers of services to the consumers of those services. It is about control over providers. So far consumer appraisal has been aimed at measuring the levels of provision, not the effectiveness of the individual.

Pollitt indicates that managerial models seeem to be the most common.

Even so, we might expect that systems of appraisal will be transparent and will ensure that individuals are rewarded on the basis of merit. We would not expect the reward process to be used to make budget savings, put pressure on staff to work harder or to punish individuals because of personality conflicts (see Douglas 1996). Individuals must be informed of what is expected of them and be given the appropriate training to carry out the tasks set.

Winstanley and Stuart-Smith (1996) argue that four ethical principles need to be built into the process of performance appraisal and these are:

1 Respect for the individual.
2 Mutual respect.
3 Procedural fairness.
4 Transparency of decision-making.

They are critical of performance measurement in so far as there is no evidence that improved performance results! They identify five critiques of performance measurement:

1 Lack of success. There is no conclusive evidence that the use of performance measurement systems actually improves performance.
2 Problems in operationalizing performance measurement systems, typically referring to the difficulty of setting objectives.

3 Impact on people, stressing that performance measurement is riven with subjectivity and bias. We examine this below.
4 The exercise of power and control through a performance measurement system, again examined below.
5 Assumption of a unitarist organizational framework. As we have already indicated a multiple stakeholder approach is appropriate.

In performance measurement there is a need to canvass the views of the marginalized. Evaluators make the error of assuming the interests of the institution as a whole are the same as the interests of senior managers and officials.

In theory, performance appraisal is an objective, rational and systematic attempt on the part of managers to accurately describe the performance of subordinates based upon a set of given criteria and linked to agreed-upon objectives. However, as Longenecker and Ludwig (1990) argue there may be a number of reasons why appraisal reflects bias.

1 Reasons for inflating ratings
   ● A damaging effect on morale.
   ● To avoid airing dirty washing in public.
   ● To protect good performers whose work may have temporarily suffered.
   ● To get rid of colleagues who underperform.
2 Reasons for lowering ratings
   ● To 'jolt' staff into better performance.
   ● To punish a difficult subordinate.
   ● To encourage a problem employee to quit.
   ● To comply with an organizational edict that forbids high marks.

For the above reasons, trust, which should be at the heart of managerial relations, may go out of the window when performance appraisal is at stake unless the processes are transparent and procedural justice is seen to exist.

Performance and control

McKevitt and Lawton (1996) examined a multi-stakeholder approach to performance measurement, based on the typology offered by Kanter and Summers (1987), discussed in the previous section, and discovered that a top-down approach to performance measures fails to engage middle manager commitment and as a result performance measures are not embedded in organizations. Performance measurement appears to have been used as a top-down instrument of senior management control in both central and local government. However, such power and control will not be given up lightly. McKevitt and Lawton (1996: 51) found that:

The service delivered is based on normative need, as perceived by the professional service deliverer, rather than on need felt or expressed by the client ... finding a suitable, feasible and acceptable way of introducing client-based performance assessment is not easy. In particular those who have strong professional allegiances will inevitably feel that these may be compromised by being influenced by customers.

Performance indicators tend to be dominated by the demands of more powerful stakeholders, notably central government, senior managers or professionals. Front-line managers and clients or users have virtually no input. This reflects a command and control, top-down, model of implementation. Performance measurement is a political and value-laden process and implementation issues are crucial. Carter (1989) argued that performance indicators provided the opportunity for government to retain firm control over departments by exercising a strategy of 'hands off' rather than 'hands on' control. Such a strategy, Carter argued, helped fill the accountability gap left by the creation of agencies. In the area of performance appraisal Madron (1995: 187) also emphasizes the control dimension and makes the point that: '... PRP [performance-related pay] and the accompanying appraisal systems are intended to act as instruments of compulsion to enforce obedience and eliminate any sense of mutual obligation between employees'.

Conclusion

We have argued both in this chapter and in Chapter 1 that ethics within organizations operate at different levels and returned to some of the issues that this raises within the context of evaluation. You will recall that theorists such as Fukuyama (1995) examined the development of trust through the 'social capital' created by institutions within society. A crucial question is the extent to which individuals are capable of putting aside their individual self-interests and joining together in shared undertakings whether they be in business, the church, educational institutions, state institutions or whatever. This is the issue addressed by Sir Geoffrey Vickers in his search for 'the spirit of administration' (1965). Vickers saw institutions as the necessary means of social regulation. He argues that it is not so much goals that we seek as the maintenance of relationships; we recognize our interdependence and the inescapability of social regulation. He would have little time for the rationality of performance measurement. He recognizes the existence of individual autonomy but argues that it takes place within a context. Regulation is not conceived as a Hobbesian contract but more of a bond, a multi-tiered structure of interdependencies. It is conceived not as an externally generated set of rules but as a continuous process of establishing and maintaining order in societies and the relationships between individuals (see Johnson 1994): it is the relationships that hold us together far more than the goals to be achieved!

> Whether we are considering political institutions such as a cabinet or a parliamentary select committee, legal institutions such as a court of appeal or a magistrate's court, educational institutions such as a university or a comprehensive school, advisory institutions such as a royal commission, administrative institutions such as the civil service or some other public bureaucratic organization, in all these and countless other cases what is crucial to the definition of the institution is how it operates rather than what it actually achieves. For it is by establishing relationships that an institution makes a contribution to the ongoing regulation of society. And all serious arguments about institutions are for this reason ultimately arguments about changing the relationships that they sustain.
>
> (Johnson 1994: 39)

There is a sense in which we live in 'the evaluative state' where the prevailing ethos is 'If it moves measure it!' We appear to be overwhelmingly goal-oriented and procedural issues and processes are downgraded. In so doing the quality of relationships within organizational life and the feelings of mutual trust and obligations and reciprocal rights and responsibilities are lost. Instead we have the fragmentation of responsibility throughout organizations but often without power or authority. Notions such as 'freedom to manage' and 'empowerment' are passed off as liberating tools but could also be seen as increasing the pressures that organizations exert upon individuals.

We agree with the observation made by Wanna *et al.* (1992: 216) that: '... public sector accountability is an ongoing obligation and relationship of trust, not simply a performance contract maintained by annual bottom-line results'.

eight

Ethical training
for decisions

Key issues

- The extent to which ethics can be taught.
- The ways in which ethics training can help managers to make practical decisions.
- The relationship between individual, organizational and societal learning.

Introduction

It has become a cliché that people are an organization's most valued resource. As one senior manager in New South Wales government put it: 'The trick is to tap hidden talents, to give them an opportunity' (personal interview, September 1994). For this to have any meaning, employees must be treated as individuals and not as a means to some organizational end. Such an argument will apply to any organization irrespective of whether it is in the public or private sector. Thus, for example, in her book on business ethics, Sternberg (1994) argues from the point of view of distributive justice that employees should be rewarded according to their contribution to enhancing the value of the company. Of course, this is not always straightforward as is assumed, since who owns performance is not always clear. However, Sternberg contends that:

> Treating employees ethically simply means treating them with ordinary decency and distributive justice. The ethical business rewards contributions to the business objective, and is honest and fair to its staff; it avoids lying, cheating and stealing, coercion, physical violence and

illegality. And crucially, since trust is so dependent upon expectations, the ethical business is extremely careful about the expectations it engenders.

(1994: 125)

Ethical business, according to this argument, is built upon relationships. Ethical activity is concerned with human activity and so is business. From this perspective, bad ethics is bad business: customers, suppliers or employees all ultimately leave. This is the first strand to the ethical framework in training: the organizational context within which training takes place and, as we saw in Chapter 6, to how an organization treats its staff.

The second strand is concerned with what the organization does. It is no good an organization taking seriously the equal opportunities of its staff, for example, if at the same time it exploits a minority group through its services or products. And vice versa: claims that an organization is promoting the common welfare will be undermined if it treats its own staff appallingly. Thus this chapter examines the need for ethics training at the individual and the organizational level.

Of course, as we saw in our discussion of codes of conduct, not everyone will see the need for such training nor agree about what such a training might consist of. Jackson (1993) illustrates the difficulties in creating ethics courses for public managers and refers to the long-standing belief that the effective public services manager 'requires nothing more than diligence and common sense' (p. 34). This view is becoming increasingly questioned. For example, the Public Services Commission of the Australian public service runs a course for senior executive officers, part of which is laid out in Box 8.1.

Box 8.1 Managing ethically: applying Australian public service principles

Objectives
This module will help participants to:

1 Improve their understanding of the current APS environment and the place of ethical conduct in that environment.
2 Identify key principles and values that underlie ethical conduct in the public sector.
3 Improve understanding of the ethical dimension to decision-making and appropriate behaviour for public sector managers.
4 Identify the ethical issues that are likely to arise, and appropriate approaches for handling such issues.
5 Explore ways in which ethical conduct may be enhanced, and whether present guidelines and structures are sufficient to help people recognize and solve ethical problems.

The Australian public service takes the view that 'improving understanding, identifying key principles and values, adopting appropriate behaviour, recognising and solving ethical issues' are important tasks (Management Advisory Board 1996). Catron and Denhardt (1994) illustrate the range of ethics courses in the USA and identify the aims of such courses as being to:

- develop an awareness of ethical issues and problems;
- build analytical skills in ethical decision-making;
- cultivate an attitude of duty and personal responsibility in pursuing a career in the public service;
- stimulate the moral imagination;
- recognize the discretionary power of the administrator's role;
- cultivate moral character and foster ethical conduct in the public service;
- become familiar with Western traditions in moral philosophy and political thought;
- gain knowledge of the ethical standards of public administration;
- build a capacity to tolerate ambiguity and differences of opinion;
- develop a practical understanding of the constraints and expectations of administration expressed through codes of conduct, rules and norms;
- train to become an ethical leader.

Such courses are designed to promote knowledge and understanding, enhance decision-making capacity and develop the ethical behaviour of others within the organization. However, in recognizing the interplay between knowledge, understanding and action, Lilla (1981) argues that training in ethical theories is not enough. Students applying different moral theories to a public policy problem, in much the same way that we might apply a mathematical model, is deterministic and limited. According to Lilla the application of ethical theories reflects a very limited conception of ethics and of moral education: '. . . the moral life of the public official is made up of much more than the catastrophic cases which call for immediate decisions. It is made up of a set of virtues which the official has acquired throughout this education and it reveals itself in the attitudes and habits he [*sic*] displays towards the political process and the public in his day-to-day work' (p. 13).

We recognize that ethical decision-making is not just a technical exercise. At the same time however, the manager has to make decisions in the short term, often with incomplete information and little time. In the next section we offer, in the context of higher education, a set of decision trees to aid the manager in making short-term decisions.

Ethical decisions in the short term

Ethical behaviour could be promoted through education and training. In the first instance, however, the manager may need guidance in making decisions that require immediacy; as we have discussed in an earlier chapter, the manager is driven by the day-to-day. Notwithstanding that, a set of guidelines could be useful. One such set of guidelines could be provided through a decision tree and through providing decision models to be used when faced with difficult decisions. One such model is supplied by Nash (1981) who provides a set of eleven questions to guide the decision-making of managers:

1 Have you defined the problem accurately?
2 How would you define the problem if you stood on the other side of the fence?
3 How did the situation occur in the first place?
4 To whom and to what do you give your loyalty as a person and as a member of the organization?
5 What is your intention in making this decision?
6 How does the intention compare with the probable result?
7 Whom would your decision or action injure?
8 Can you discuss the problem with the affected parties before you make your decision?
9 Are you confident that your decision will be as valid over a long period of time as it is now?
10 Could you discuss, without qualms, your decision with your boss, your chief executive officer, your family, society as a whole?
11 Under what circumstances would you allow exceptions to your stand?

The responses to such questions will require more than the consultation of a code of conduct. They will depend upon the extent to which the individuals have internalized the principles upon which codes are built and the extent to which codes are embedded within the organizational cultures. At the same time, some issues do not lend themselves easily to such decision processes. Kernaghan (1993) argues that, in discussing public service ethics:

1 Written ethical rules in general and codes of ethics in particular are an important but insufficient means of promoting public service ethics.
2 Certain ethical issues are more amenable to management than others. For example, it might be easier to have a set of rules to manage conflicts of interest than to manage 'promoting the public interest'.

The case study shows how one university is providing an ethical framework for its staff.

Case study: Ethical decisions in higher education

There are increasing pressures on resources and on student numbers facing higher education institutions in an increasingly competitive marketplace. At present, many universities have a range of courses on offer, for undergraduate and postgraduate students, and for students working towards management certificates and diplomas. These are taught on a full-time, part-time and on an open and distance learning basis. Many universities are seeking to expand their numbers by recruiting from both home and abroad and are seeking to attract corporate clients by offering tailor-made courses. This is particularly true in business studies and management disciplines. This case examines how a (fictional) university, Borrowton University, might encounter ethical problems and how these might be dealt with. The university has a prestigious, world-renowned, business school which offers a range of first-degree, postgraduate and professional qualifications, and is expanding its distance learning operations. Because of its prestige and success it is being courted by organizations at home and abroad to provide management development programmes and qualifications and has also been approached by universities abroad to take part in collaborative arrangements. The university has a very clear mission statement which incorporates an equal opportunities statement:

> We are a university that welcomes and encourages staff and students to participate fully and equally in all our activities. We are creating and maintaining conditions where students and staff are treated solely on the basis of their merits, ability and potential, regardless of gender, colour, ethnic or national origin, age, socioeconomic background, disability, religious or political beliefs, family circumstances, sexual orientation or other irrelevant distinction.

In addition the business school has an international strategy document which has three strands to it:

1 Academic integrity.
2 Operational feasibility.
3 Financial viability.

Criteria to secure academic integrity are identified as the need to maintain the integrity of the courses, acceptable assessment procedures, acceptable admission criteria and quality control through the course teams.

The university has also stated in a number of documents that it has a 'transformative role through education' to play and has been encouraged by its government to support the transformation of regimes overseas through its educational programmes.

The business school has expanded rapidly and is seen as a 'cash cow' by the university. It is driven by the need to increase numbers, and hence income, in a very competitive market. Most of its courses are 'full cost' (i.e. the student or organization pays the full cost of the course and there are no government grants or subsidies) and the business school generates a healthy revenue. However, there are concerns being expressed by staff within the school that income generation is becoming its prime motive at the expense of its educational goals. Increasing pressures are felt by staff who feel that the operational feasibility of offering courses in other countries puts them under tremendous strain and that decisions are being taken purely on financial grounds.

The business school was recently approached by the government of a foreign country to provide management development courses for senior civil servants and government ministers. This government had recently been criticized in the international press for its treatment of dissidents and its human rights record. At the same time the business school had recently agreed to provide management development for middle and senior managers in a large multinational company in a very lucrative deal. However, it became apparent during the first year of this course that the multinational company was making excessive demands on the business school, requiring preferential treatment, extra tutoring above the norm and an input into assessment practices. Some staff in the business school were being put under extra pressure and felt that decisions were being taken which bypassed the usual channels that maintained academic integrity. At a monthly meeting of the business school board the pressures began to show and a very heated discussion took place with some members of staff arguing that financial considerations were driving out other considerations and that the university's mission was being undermined. Others felt that on ethical grounds the business school was entering into negotiations with what they considered to be dubious regimes and with companies whose record on corporate social responsibility left a lot to be desired. Still others felt that some of these negotiations were being held in secret, that the tradition of openness was being undermined and that staff who were having to cope with these new corporate clients were being put under tremendous pressure to allow special treatment. The business school decided to set up an ethics sub-commitee to examine these issues and to report back with a series of recommendations to ensure that the business school took account of the ethical dimensions of its work. After much deliberation, heated discussion and the general feeling of walking on quicksand, the sub-committee identified three domains for its deliberations: the international, the corporate and the individual. The committee recognized that any proposals must be consistent with both the university's mission statement and the business school's strategy. It also recognized that any set of guidelines must offer practical advice and it recommended a set of short-term and long-term proposals. It recognized that many of the issues raised are not easily resolvable. However, it felt that in offering a set of guidelines then any decisions taken concerning the school's future activities would have considered the ethical implications of those decisions. The committee was concerned to offer a practical set of guidelines concerning who it did business with, in what ways and how responsibilities were shared out. As a practical guide the committee came up with a set of decision trees to help guide decisions:

Domain 1: the international domain

A range of issues were identified which included:

- The nature of the regime with which the proposal was concerned.
- The role of education as a 'liberating' or transforming vehicle.
- The need to recognize and reconcile different ethical practices and competing value systems.

Question 1
Is a minority group being systematically deprived of its human rights by the majority such that:

(a) The regime has been condemned in the international arena by bodies such as the UN.
(b) The business school's courses would not be made available to minority groups within the country because of systematic discrimination of the form outlined in the university's mission statement?

If the answer to either (a) or (b) is YES then answer Question 2 if NO then move on to Question 3.

Question 2
Could the adoption of the business school's courses lead to the creation of living and working conditions where human rights can be respected without prejudice?

YES   move on to Question 3   NO   do not proceed
If the answer is DON'T KNOW then seek further information and assurances from all relevant stakeholders.

Question 3
In being associated with such a country is unfavourable publicity likely to result?
NO   move on to Question 4   YES   do not proceed

Question 4
Can the business school's education standards be maintained while being harmonized with the needs and capabilities of the client?
YES   then proceed   NO   do not proceed

The committee thought about drawing up a list of countries which are on the 'black lists' of international groups and its own government. The nature of such lists, however, appeared to be arbitrary and be open to the charge of hypocrisy. Thus, from a UK perspective, how does Northern Ireland fit in? From an Australian perspective, should its treatment of Aborigines be an issue?

Domain 2: the corporate domain

The issues identified included:

● Preferential treatment given to corporate customers.
● Threats posed to academic integrity.
● Relationships with multinational corporations.

The committee resisted the temptation to provide blacklists in terms of a companies' support for regimes with: a poor human rights record; their exploitation of resources both natural and human; unethical practices in terms of product development, manufacturing processes or 'dumping' of products.

Question 1
Does the organization have a set of values that are consistent with the university's mission statement?
YES   move to Question 4   NO   move to Question 2

Question 2
Does the organization respect the philosophy of the university?
YES   move to Question 3   NO   do not proceed

Question 3
Is the organization willing to work to achieve the same standards, for example, in equal opportunities?
YES   move to Question 4   NO   do not proceed

Question 4
Is the organization seeking favourable treatment from the business school in ways that might discriminate against business school staff and other students?
YES   move to Question 5   NO   move to Question 6

Question 5
Does the organization recognize the consequences of its requirements and is it willing to temper those requirements?
YES   move to Question 6   NO   do not proceed

Question 6
Has the course team been informed of any special demands and is it willing to respond?
YES   move to Question 7   NO   consult with course team

Question 7
Is the organization willing to subscribe to exclusion clauses such that the material would not be used in certain countries or would seek the business school's approval if the material is to be used other than specified in the original agreement?
YES   move to Question 8   NO   do not proceed

Question 8
Have the costs in human terms been calculated? Is the timetable a reasonable one?
YES   move to Question 9   NO   discuss with resource holders

Question 9
Has the business school clearly specified that, in educational matters, responsibility is to the student and that this includes confidentiality?
YES   move to Question 10   NO   clarify with the organization

Question 10
Have all the issues been resolved before signing the contract?
YES   move to Question 11   NO   revisit Questions 1–9

Question 11
Would you feel comfortable if the outcome is exposed to a wider audience e.g. the university as a whole?
YES   proceed   NO   do not proceed

Domain 3: the individual

The issues identified were:

- Personal integrity.
- Professional excellence.
- Treatment of others.
- Relationships with outside stakeholders.
- Promotion of an ethical organization.

Question 1
Have you examined the issue from the perspective of others involved?
YES   move to Question 2   NO   reconsider

Question 2
Is your decision consistent with the university and the business school's philosophy and values?
YES   move to Question 3   NO   reconsider

Question 3
Would you feel comfortable if your action is exposed to a wider audience?
YES   move to Question 4   NO   reconsider

Question 4
Have you discussed the issue with the relevant stakeholders?
YES   move to Question 5   NO   gain the view of all those affected

Question 5
Does a decision result in extra work for staff?
YES   proceed to Question 6   NO   proceed

Question 6
Have staff agreed to the extra work?
YES   proceed   NO   do not proceed

The committee argued that if the above decision trees were used before making any commitments, then the business school would not be in a position of having to deliver a course that it did not feel comfortable with and was not consistent with the university and the business school's philosophy. The school would be helped in this if the school's processes were such that:

- The discussions were transparent.
- Relevant stakeholders had been consulted.
- Quality was assured through assessment procedures that all courses had adopted.
- There was openness in terms of who was to be involved in any special projects involving other countries or corporate clients.

The committee recognized that there would be considerable overlap between the three domains and that they should be taken as a whole. The committee recommended that the business school adopt the guidelines as described above. In the longer term the school should seek to raise ethical awareness among all its staff through a series of workshops with the support of senior staff. The committee argued that raising ethical awareness was part of a learning process and was iterative in nature. One of the outcomes of such a development programme may be a code of conduct. At this stage the committee was concerned that the business school treated staff and students with respect, adopted practices that were consistent with the university and the school's philosophy and values, and were keenly aware of how decisions taken were likely to affect others.

What are the ethical issues raised through the use of decision trees such as those presented in the case study?

- Cultural relativism and the extent to which values can, and should be, transplanted elsewhere through educational programmes.
- Corporate social responsibility and the obligations of large organizations to their customers and their own staff.
- Partnership with the private sector and the extent to which practices acceptable in one sphere are acceptable in another.

- Academic integrity versus other values such as financial viability.
- Organizational versus individual values.

Note that there is the *Code of Practice for Overseas Collaborative Provision in Higher Education* (Higher Education Quality Council 1996) which states that its role is: '. . . to offer informed advice on the difficult task of ensuring that the quality and standards of the awards and programmes provided through partnerships with overseas institutions of higher education are comparable with those available at partner institutions within the UK' (p. 3). The code of practice covers: purposes, responsibility for quality and standards, selection of partners, financial arrangements and formal agreements, quality control, the use of agents, entry and certification validation, academic standards, and assessments.

However, the decisions to be taken in the short term, as in the case study, require reflection and the concept of the reflective practitioner is one that is gaining currency in management education circles. The notion of reflective practice is associated with Schön (1983), who defined reflective practice as involving the manager in a number of processes and activities:

- Accurately describing existing management practices.
- Reflecting critically on those practices.
- Reconsidering future management practices in the light of this reflection.
- Making fresh plans for future management practices on the basis of this consideration.
- Carrying out these plans.
- Continuing to reflect on and to monitor these practices.

Reflective practice requires being sensitive and self aware in practice and involves a continual process of self-monitoring, leading to growing self-awareness. It is not just empty 'navel gazing', but is concerned with activity and continous performance improvement. The kinds of questions asked in the decision tree are all part of the reflective practitioner approach. It is questioning the status quo and the organization's assumptions. Sometimes it is difficult as we are swept away by the 'here and now'. Managers need to stand back!

The moral development of the individual

One view of ethical education and training is that ethical training should focus on the individual and be concerned with the processes of ethical reasoning. Kohlberg (1976) offers us the best-known and most well-used schema which examines the individual's capacity for ethical reasoning. According to Kohlberg, people pass through three basic levels in terms of their capacity to engage in independent moral reasoning and to express a concern for the just treatment of others:

1 Pre-conventional
  - Stage 1: the pre-conventional level where individuals adopt reward-seeking and punishment-avoiding behaviour. It is self-interested behaviour and is characterized by fear and deference. From an organizational point of view, individuals at this stage are likely to follow rules without question.
  - Stage 2: characterized by a hedonistic orientation with an instrumental view of human relations and some sense of reciprocity and exchange of favours. Morality is satisfying one's interests and living up to agreements without asking too many questions. Personal gain will be maximized.

2 Conventional
  - Stage 3: a 'good person' orientation in which individuals seek to maintain expectations and win approval from a peer group. Morality is defined by individual ties and relationships. Individuals will seek to 'fit in' and get along with their peers.
  - Stage 4: conventional role-conformity where loyalty to the prevailing social order is displayed and where the importance of rules and the law is paramount. There is little recognition of discretion and a strong commitment to the organization will be displayed.

Stages 3 and 4 recognize that we take on various social roles and that this includes notions of obligations, duties, rights etc.

3 Principled or post-conventional
  - Stage 5: demonstrates an orientation to the social contract. Morality is based upon the protection of rational social utility such that social contracts are developed based upon majority interest. A utilitarian approach might be appropriate.
  - Stage 6: concerned with principled or autonomous reasoning by individuals. This also requires a commitment to values and behaviour, not just recognition of them. This could be the nature of moral judgement. Principles of justice are based upon the fundamental equal worth of individuals.

Stages 5 and 6 are where the individual transcends social conventions out of a concern for higher principles. These stages are achieved by relatively few people. An organization's staff may be at different stages of moral development and may not understand each other's point of view. Gortner (1991) argues that the idea of a hierarchy of moral maturity was generally understood by the managers that he surveyed. However, how feasible is it to expect individuals within organizations to act at Stages 5 and 6? It was argued in Chapter 4 that the location of the public service ethos, which on Kohlberg's scheme we might expect to be found at Stages 5 and 6, is best located in terms of relationships that might be located at Stages 3 and 4. If concepts of the public service ethos or the public interest are to be located at Stages 5 and 6 they will have little meaning for most managers. At the same time, however, possessing the capacity for moral reasoning does not necessarily mean that individuals will act in that way. The quality of an ethical action will be in individuals willing to take personal responsibility and having the capacity to act in support of their moral beliefs. An approach which focuses on the capacity of individuals for moral reasoning will not take account of the specific role and responsibilities of individual public managers and the organizational context.

Rohr (1978) makes a distinction between a 'low road' and a 'high road' approach to ethics. The 'low road' stresses exclusively adherence to formal rules. This type of training focuses on imparting a knowledge of departmental rules and regulations and codes of conduct. The 'high road' approach focuses on grand theory found in political and ethical philosophy, and this is too highbrow for Rohr.

Lewis (1991) distinguishes between compliance ethics and integrity ethics, each requiring different training programmes. A compliance approach is concerned with external rules and an integrity approach is concerned with internalizing rules, principles and values. This distinction is at the heart of much of the debate concerning ethics as the regulation of conduct; should regulation be externally imposed by a code of conduct? This may be necessary to ensure accountability, yet it tends to discourage public managers from performing above minimum standards. What is legal may not be right. Alternatively, an integrity approach seeks to develop understanding and judgement in order to act in an ethical manner and where ethical principles are internalized. Hejka-Ekins (1994) provides an account of training programmes which include:

- knowledge of legal requirements;
- identification of ethical standards and values;
- knowledge of the democratic ethos;
- use of moral exemplars;
- use of case studies to promote and develop ethical reasoning;
- consolidation into agency culture;
- a focus upon the organization as well as the individual;
- awareness of societal expectations including the extent of citizens' involvement and the public's views of the profession.

Such programmes focus on the individual, the organization and the society, and this is the view taken in this book: that the ethics of managers must be located within the wider environment.

The learning organization

Hejka-Ekins (1994) locates her discussion of the different approaches to ethics training in the organizational context. Her three propositions are:

1 The more bureaucratic the organization the more likely it is to use a compliance model.
2 The more democratic, flexible and open the organization, the more likely it is to use integrity ethics.
3 Organizations that have a mixture of both will have a fusion of the two.

Can organizations learn in the same way that individuals can? What is the learning organization? According to a new bulletin from the National Institute for Social Work (1997: 1):

> That work-based learning is important needs to be continuously re-stated. The 'learning organisation' is not a limp intellectual concept but a life-saving necessity. Recent reports on disasters like Zeebrugge, Hillsborough or Kings Cross, as well as verdicts on child protection failures, have repeated that the information needed to avoid these tragedies already existed inside the main organisations involved. The reports asked: where were the systems or the emotional climate necessary to spread that learning around?

Definitions of the learning organization include: 'Learning is a dynamic concept and its use in theory emphasizes the continually changing nature of organizations. Furthermore, it is an integrative concept that can unify various levels of analysis: individual, group, corporate, which is particularly helpful in reviewing the cooperative and community nature of organizations' (Dodgson 1993: 376). According to Dodgson (p. 377) the characteristics of the learning organization are:

- The activities of learning and helping others to learn are recognized and encouraged and the skills necessary for the achievement of learning are highly valued. Individual members are encouraged to learn and develop their full potential.
- Senior managers will take the lead and demonstrate that they value learning.
- The learning culture will be extended to include customers, clients and other significant stakeholders.
- The organization continually undergoes a process of transformation through reflection, generation of options and action.

Senge (1990) identifies 11 features of a learning company:

1 A learning approach to strategy such that strategy formulation, implementation and evaluation form a continuous process to be adapted in the light of experience.
2 Participative policy-making which involves a wide range of stakeholders and is an expression of a wide range of views and values.
3 'Informating' which refers to the use of information technology to empower people rather than oppress them.

4 Formative accounting and control, such that financial systems are designed to assist learning.
5 Internal exchange requires a perspective that sees all internal departments and units as customers of each other. The key is, however, collaboration rather than competition.
6 Reward flexibility which may mean changing the distributions of reward and the distributions of power.
7 Enabling structures which require flexibility.
8 Boundary workers as environmental scanners and information gatherers on customer needs.
9 Inter-company learning for mutual benefits.
10 A learning climate where senior managers give a lead in questioning their own assumptions and seeking after continuous improvement.
11 Self-development opportunities for all, encouraging people to take control and responsibility for their own learning and development.

In the learning organization, mutual learning characterizes the relationship between the individual and the organization such that individuals are socialized into organizational cultures and organizations store knowledge in the procedures, rules and norms. Whether or not individuals adjust to the organization before it has had time to learn from them is a moot point.

To what extent do public services organizations match up? Commenting upon Civil Service training Plowden (1994: 31) notes that: 'Taken as a whole, this level of training is not enough to enable a major organisation to maintain a steady state in a turbulent environment. It is not nearly enough if there is a serious intention to change organisational values, or to establish and maintain a coherent set of values in the face of increasing and outward mobility'. The Fraser Report on the UK Civil Service (Efficiency Unit 1991) suggested five days training per year for youngish Grade 7s and 5s noting that the actual figure was 0.7 days. It is also interesting to note that courses offered by the Civil Service College offer a mixture of general government frameworks, general management skills and specialist skills and knowledge, for example, in European law. Little is done in the way of ethics training. However, Argyris and Schön (1978: 3) argue that:

Organizational learning involves the detection and correction of error. When the error detected and corrected permits the organization to carry on its policies or achieve its present objectives, then that error-detection-and-correction process is single-loop learning. Double-loop learning occurs when error is detected and corrected in ways that involve the modification of an organization's underlying norms, policies and objectives.

It is only through double-loop learning that systemic corruption can be addressed, where the funadamental values and assumptions are questioned.

The OECD (1996) argues that professional socialization is the process through which public servants learn and inculcate the ethos and values of the public service. It is instructive to note that for years the Civil Service in the UK concentrated on learning on the job rather than formalized training. It may have been more appropriate than was recognized. Key socialization mechanisms are education and training programmes as well as the existence of good role models at senior levels. Professional socialization communicates standards of conduct, but, as we have argued earlier, these have to be internalized.

Suzuki (1995) examines the role of training in the Japanese police force which, he states, has an international reputation for its integrity. One main reason for this is its training programme. There is status attached to the police force and it attracts high quality candidates. All recruits, married or not, live together and share dormitory life for the full year of basic training. Close living helps develop a strong sense of group solidarity, loyalty, purpose and meaning. A system of mentoring is used, training is a continuous process, there is close cooperation between the police and the public, and shared decision-making and harmony in interpersonal relationships. Training takes account of the organizational context including management styles and involves the public.

The learning society?

In a commentary on the First Nolan report, Chapman (1995) argues that there are two considerations to ensure that ethical standards are maintained. The first is concerned with education and training for both holders of public office and for the public at large, and the second is:

> ... continuing public discussion and emphasis of the high standards that are expected. A society which fails to demand high standards in public life and which sneers and denigrates those who are doing their best in difficult circumstances in public life, cannot expect that high standards will be achieved or maintained. This is not just the reponsibility of a relatively few people in public life, but a social responsibility for everyone.
>
> (Chapman 1995: 13)

Ranson and Stewart (1994) argue for a proactive public domain which is part of the learning society. While agreeing with the sentiments expressed by Chapman (1995) and by Ranson and Stewart (1994) we need to ask how can public services organizations and managers facilitate this in practice, particularly as it is a moot point whether civil servants should determine the public interest assuming, as we discussed in Chapter 4, that its location is not always easy to find. However, we do expect public services organizations to fulfil public roles in terms of the provision of welfare, health, security and so on. According to Ranson and Stewart, management should support and express the political process. It should '. . . seek to strengthen both access to the arena of public discourse and discourse within it' (p. 107). Ranson and Stewart locate their arguments within the democratic context, both participatory and representative. They argue that government has four different roles within society:

1 A sustaining role where government supports the framework of law and order.
2 A maintenance role which provides the social and economic fabric of society.
3 A responsive role, responding to change.
4 A development role where government itself is the means of achieving change through, for example, the promotion of the good society.

Democracy is seen as an educative force, not just a system of government, which involves participation by a multiplicity of stakeholders. Ranson and Stewart (1994) argue for a learning public domain through strengthening and widening access to the arena of public discourse. However, the question of why the public should be interested in political life or citizenship is not proven! Ranson and Stewart indicate the mechanisms that can be used to facilitate public involvement including issue panels, citizen panels, community councils, user forums and so on. In a similar fashion Osborne and Gaebler list, and provide examples of, 17 different ways that the voice of the customer can be listened to (1992, see pp. 177–9):

1 Customer surveys.
2 Customer follow-ups to see if the desired results were actually achieved.
3 Community surveys.
4 Customer contact through front-line staff.
5 Customer contact reports.
6 Customer councils.
7 Focus groups which bring customers together to discuss specific services or issues.
8 Customer interviews.
9 The use of electronic mail to communicate directly.
10 Customer-service training.
11 Test marketing through piloting new services.
12 Quality guarantees.
13 Using anonymous inspectors to carry out spot checks.
14 The use of an independent ombudsman to deal with complaints.
15 Complaint tracking systems to improve response times.
16 The use of hotlines.
17 Suggestion boxes on official forms.

While such suggestions are laudable they seem to be limited in scope. They are invariably concerned with the citizen as customer and as we argued in Chapter 5 that is just one of the ways in which individuals relate to the public services. Such suggestions are concerned with the rights or entitlements of citizens in their capacities as customers. There should also be a recognition that citizens have duties. For example, those working in further and higher education are only too aware of the increase in the evaluation of lecturer performance including that evaluation made by students. At the same time it is often ovelooked that students themselves have certain responsibilities and duties: to attend, to prepare for lessons, to hand work in on time, to treat each other's ideas and opinions with respect and so on. Duties and rights are, in this sense, correlative and are part of a two-way relationship. In autumn 1997 it was announced by the government that it will rewrite the *Patients Charter* to include duties as well as rights.

Conclusion

From the above discussion we can see that ethics training can take a number of forms and be made up of a number of different elements. Above all, however, we need to be aware that intellectual understanding does not necessarily translate into action. As we discussed in our case study of the decision trees used by Borrowton University at the beginning of the chapter, managers have to make decisions based upon their reflections and guided by an ethical framework. An ethics training course, then, might contain the elements shown in Box 8.2.

Box 8.2 Ethics training for public services managers: reconciling the experiences of public services management with the insights of ethical frameworks

A. Public services management

Context
1 Knowledge of relevant legislation
2 Understanding of societal values
3 Understanding the role of public services in society
4 Appreciation of the role of public services elsewhere
5 Acknowledging the expectations of citizens

B. Ethical frameworks

Theory
1 An understanding of different theories
2 Developing ethical principles for managing public services

The formal organization	**Issues**
1 Knowledge of formal rules	1 Listening to the concerns of
2 Awareness of the processes of	employees
accountability	2 Recognizing the views of all
3 Acceptance of individual and group	stakeholders
responsibility	3 Knowledge of public service
4 Recognizing organizational concerns	concerns with integrity,
with loyalty, commitment,	impartiality and honesty
efficiency and effectiveness	
The informal organization	**Action**
1 Recognizing the values of sub-	1 Acting with respect to obligations
groups, particularly professionals	and duties against a background
2 Identifying the locations of power	of trust
3 Awareness of different management	2 Acting with due regard to both
practices in different parts of the	process and outcome, reconciling
organization	means and ends
4 Recognizing the power of culture	
and traditions	

In developing a framework for ethics training the commitment of senior management is crucial. Unless they are shown to be serious and have a sense of ownership why should those lower down in the organization bother? Not only that but due attention will need to be paid to implementation. Too often codes of conduct or equal opportunities policies are left gathering dust on office shelves. Ethics will need to be built into the decision-making processes of the organization, in the first instance by making those processes transparent.

nine

Conclusions

Managing in the public services is characterized by ambiguity in terms of goals, responsibilities, functions or relationships. It is inevitable that such ambiguity should exist given the tensions that the public services manager has to cope with. These tensions include:

- The tension between the need for control and the need for discretion.
- The tensions in managing the needs of different stakeholders.
- The requirements to provide an efficient and effective service within tight public expenditure controls and the need to respond to the rise in expectations from consumers and clients.
- The tensions in responding to changing circumstances and, at the same time, maintaining existing standards expressed in terms of accountability, honesty, integrity and duty.
- The tension between managing the daily task and maintaining a sense of self and personal integrity.

Despite fears that changes in the tasks of public services management and the conditions under which they manage will have an adverse impact on existing standards of behaviour, there is little evidence to demonstrate this. There is evidence, discussed in Chapter 2, uncovered by the Audit Commission and the Committee of Public Accounts, of fraud, conflicts of interest and maladministration but whether such instances are on the increase or whether we are more effective at uncovering them is a moot point. It is also the case that fraud can be identified and legislated against; it will be less easy to uncover examples of lack of courtesy or respect. However, it is worth recalling that fraud, corruption and conflicts of interest in the public services were investigated in the 1970s by the Redcliffe-Maud Committee (1979) and by the Royal Commission on Standards of Conduct in Public Life chaired by Lord Salmon (1976).

Notwithstanding that, we indicated in Chapter 1 that there are a number of imperatives that affect not just the context of public services management but also the day-to-day activity of managers. For example, the fragmentation imperative is not just about creating business units or cost centres but is also concerned with devolving responsibility; the audit or performance imperative raises questions concerning the use to which performance measures are put; the efficiency imperative may put pressure on middle managers to respond to the resource constraints imposed by senior management and to the raised expectations of better quality services from clients.

We have argued that a concern with public service ethics should not be confined to specific examples of corrupt behaviour or fraudulent activity but should also examine the purpose of government, the impact of organizations on their staff, the nature of individual behaviour and relations between different stakeholders, the ethos of those that work in the public services and the ethical principles that might underpin that ethos.

The purpose of government

As we discussed in Chapter 1, government can have an economic purpose in providing public goods. Government has provided an alternative to the market as an allocator of resources. In different places and at different times, governments have played other roles. As Downie (1964: 73) puts it: 'It is by means of governmental activity that the public good can most adequately be served, for the superior power of the government makes it in most cases an incomparably better vehicle for that end than any one person or group'.

The concept of the public good is, of course, open to debate. Not only that but, from an ethical perspective, the scale of the activity may be less important than the content and scope. To what extent are there basic values necessary for any society to survive and flourish? Bok (1995) argues that every society has formulated certain values which express some form of mutual support, loyalty, affection and reciprocity. At the same time, Bok argues, all societies have basic injunctions against force or violence, fraud and deceit, and these injunctions will be supported by constraints on the breach of promises and contracts made. Along with a rudimentary form of procedural justice, this, according to Bok, makes up the basis of a minimalist framework of ethics for any society. Bok argues that taking these values seriously is indispensable for a common life and that this is based upon trust. This is the same argument that Fukuyama (1995) puts forward. This raises the question of the role of the public services manager in promoting the social cohesion that underpins a common life and the argument put forward in this book is that this is done through the manner in which those working in the public services conduct their relationships with a range of different stakeholders. That conduct is underpinned by traditions and organizational and professional cultures and practices. This is not to say that the balance between ends and means, between implementing public policy through relationships with clients, users, patients or citizens, is an easy one to maintain.

Bok (1995) argues that the values described above can be used as a basis for understanding and passing judgement across cultural boundaries, while still respecting cultural diversity. These values can inform a common dialogue about how best to cope with military, environmental or other hazards that do not respect national frontiers. The concern with corruption, bribery and fraud is universal. Gilman and Lewis (1996) indicate that more and more countries are putting structural arrangements in place, in the form of inspector generals or ombudsmen, to combat corruption. Gilman and Lewis also argue for a global dialogue on ethical issues.

However, while such developments are laudable, we have argued that ethics within the public services is not just concerned with the high profile public cases but is also concerned with how organizations treat their staff and how staff treat each other and their clients or consumers. The grounding for ethics in the public services is in how services are delivered and not just what is delivered. Indeed, it can be argued that in many parts of the public service the product is the service and to treat clients with dignity and respect is the nature of the task.

Theory and practice

Principles of ethics are derived from more general social and ethical theories. A genuinely shared morality requires a justification in a shared conception of the purpose and meaning of human life. Without such a justification it is difficult to resolve competing ethical claims. Ethical dilemmas arise in particular situations: the promotion of choice for one individual may limit that of another individual. Utilitarianism offers one solution and this was discussed in Chapter 3. In practice we prioritize, and our choices will be conditioned by a number of factors rooted in a particular society at a particular time and in a particular practice.

Ethical principles are not just expressions of value, but judgements of right and wrong. The theories that we examined in Chapter 3 were concerned with both ends and means. However, in the public services one does not preclude the other; as we suggested above, the two are inextricably linked.

The link between theory and practice is the link between knowing and acting. As we indicated in Chapter 3, values are given expression in principles which are put into practice through the exercise of virtues. Moral action is a matter of engagement which requires a disposition to act. Of course this is not a logical sequence of events but is iterative in nature. In his study Watson (1996) found that the actions of managers are shaped by sets of beliefs and generalizations which involve a mixture of pragmatic and ethical principles. However, 'espoused' theories are different from the theories in use. For the manager, theories inform but do not direct behaviour and this is consistent with the view taken in this book that ethical frameworks can act as guidelines. According to Watson, managers often do not act in ways that they claim to! Managers may discover a theory but not apply it; they may not even be able to articulate it. Therefore, research based solely on managers' accounts of what they do is necessary but not sufficient. We need to analyse how they act, through, for example, participant observation.

Obligations and relationships

Individuals incur a range of obligations. Citizens who take part in a community engage with that community. To argue that an individual who belongs to a community voluntarily and enjoys the benefits on offer does not have any obligations to other members of that community is perverse. Individuals will have other obligations, both general and specific, arising out of the different roles they play in their personal and professional lives.

Obligations arise as a result of being a public official and specific obligations arise as a result of being a social worker or a policy adviser depending upon the particular role that is played. Obligations will exist at different levels. This is one of the features of working in the public services. Thus a solicitor working in the private sector has a duty to the client but not to society as a whole other than to be honest which is part of the even more general obligation of citizenship.

Professionalism is concerned with the suspension of self-interest: professionals must place themselves in the clients position out of a sense of duty. At the same time there may be benefits internal to the practice itself; there is an intrinsic excellence in being a professional which is concerned with the satisfaction of doing a job to the best of one's professional ability and being recognized by peers and colleagues.

We have argued that the public services depend upon satisfactory relationships between a range of stakeholders and these relationships will be based on trust. There is nothing new in this argument. As we have seen Fukuyama (1995) used it in the context of society and the economy at large and Barnard (1938) has argued that relationships within complex organizations follow the same cooperative relations as those between individuals. Cooperation depends upon each individual achieving a satisfactory balance of advantages over disadvantages. Such advantages, or incentives as Barnard calls them, will also include the satisfaction of personal ideals such as pride in craftsmanship or in achieving the goals of the organization.

Ethical enforcement

A great deal of the interest in public service ethics is as much to do with illegal behaviour as immoral behaviour. There is a powerful tradition in legal philosophy, the 'natural law' tradition, that sees law as grounded in something external to itself i.e. a system of ethics. Within this tradition there is a necessary relationship between the law and morals. The view taken in this book is that the relationship is necessary but not sufficient. We have examined the importance of codes in the regulation of behaviour and found them wanting not least because their enforcement is often lacking. It is interesting to note that there appears to be an increase in malpractice suits against professionals and this may, in part, be due to the failure of professionals to regulate themselves. If there is no trust in the process of investigating complaints of unprofessional behaviour then enforcement is weakened and malpractice suits follow.

Professional codes which have traditionally formed much of the enforcement context in the public services require self-regulation. This has often been guaranteed as professionals internalize the values that codes express. Problems arise if professionals and their values are devalued and undermined. What takes the place of the professional judgement and the integrity of, say, the teacher? Chapter 7 discussed the problems associated with the increased use of unsuitable performance measures as a form of control. Internalizing professional values is one of the objectives of ethics training courses. We can distinguish between the ethics of abiding by rules and an ethics of responsibility. The former will rely on legislation and on management controls and the latter will rely on a sense of personal responsibility based on professionalism or a commitment to public service. Figure 9.1 illustrates the difference and locates statutory codes of conduct and professional judgement on the grid.

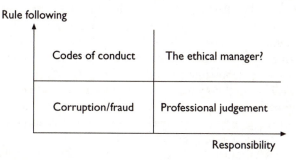

Figure 9.1 Rule following and discretion

Traditions and practices

Organizations develop their own controls and it is difficult for professionals to have complete autonomy. These controls are found in the informal traditions and practices of an organization as much as in its formal rules. The notion of empowerment involves senior management giving up power, and therefore control, to others usually lower down the organization. This is one of the tensions between control and autonomy.

However, the ethical fabric of an organization will consist of traditions and practices enshrined in organizational memories. How organizations treat their staff will reflect these traditions and practices. The relationship between the organization and the individual will vary according to the purposes of the organization and the reasons that people have for working in that organization. In the public services (characterized as bureaucratic) psychological studies of the bureaucratic personality have been attempted. There appears to be little compelling evidence to suggest that bureaucrats are any different from any other type of worker. This is not surprising when we consider that most large organizations consist of subcultures and occupational communities. Organizations are dynamic, performing different functions through different means. It was this argument, presented in Chapter 4, that explained the difficulties in locating a public service ethos that applied across the public services as a whole.

Learning, evaluation and ethics

Managers need guidance to help them make difficult decisions in specific circumstances. This guidance could be linked to outcomes – that is, providing some indication of who benefits and who loses from a decision. It could also be linked to process – that is, how a decision is made and implemented may have ethical implications. Chapter 8 provided an example of a case using a decision tree, yet in the long term we argued that guidance is linked to organizational and individual learning.

Organizations store knowledge in their procedures, norms and rules which is accumulated over time. Part of the task of the manager is utilizing and learning from that accumulated store of wisdom. Organizations who dispense with that accumulated store of knowledge and wisdom wholesale through 'downsizing' do so at their peril! This is where performance appraisal is difficult. How is it possible to evaluate the performance of a policy adviser whose skill lies in 'knowing the politician's mind' and knowing the 'rules of the game'? At the risk of repetition it is easier to evaluate the product rather than the process, particularly when, as we discussed in Chapter 7, it is difficult to ascribe responsibility.

However, ethical issues within organizations end with individuals. As Dobel (1990: 358) argues:

At a minimum, maintaining personal integrity and responsibility in public service means that individuals may not impute to others or to institutional structures the full responsibility for actions they perform and the outcomes to which they contribute. No rules or strict orders totally exonerate them from outcomes to which they contribute and which they judge as immoral, illegal or wasteful. As such they should be subject to praise and blame, guilt, shame, or satisfaction for such actions.

Ethical issues are all around those who work in organizations, whether we recognize them or not, by virtue of the fact that they work in such environments and have relationships with their colleagues. Not only that but those working in the public services are working within organizations which exist to fulfil social and ethical purposes. While accepting that organizations have a history and a fabric made up of practices and traditions that are greater than the sum of the individuals working within them at any one time, it is still individuals acting on behalf of organizations that make decisions concerning other individuals. We cannot hide behind roles: if we are told by a senior manager to massage statistics, to bend the rules in favour of one client or contractor, to dilute the quality of what we produce because of the demands of cost-cutting, we can take a stand. Individuals can make a difference. Whistleblowing might be an extreme act but individuals can retain personal and professional integrity in the face of increasing demands placed upon them. It is not easy but individuals have to live with the consequences of their actions; they have to be willing to expose their decisions to public scrutiny and be comfortable with the actions that they have taken. It is here that theory is tested out.

References

Albin, S. (1995) Managerializing local government, in S. Rees and G. Rodley (eds) *The Human Costs of Managerialism*. Leichhardt, Australia: Pluto Press.

Allison, G.T. (1983) Public and private management: are they fundamentally alike in all unimportant respects? in J.L. Perry and K.L. Kraemer (eds) *Public Management: Public and Private Perspectives*. Palo Alto, CA: Mayfield Publishing Company.

Anechiarico, F. and Jacobs, J.B. (1994) Visions of corruption control and the evolution of American public administration. *Public Administration Review*, 45 (5): 465–73.

Argyris, C. and Schön, D. (1978) *Organizational Learning: A Theory of Action Perspective*. Reading, MA: Addison-Wesley.

Armstrong, R. (1985) Note of guidance, *The Duties and Responsibilities of Civil Servants in Relation to Ministers*. London: Cabinet Office.

Arrow, K. (1974) *The Limits of Organization*. New York: Norton & Co.

Audit Commission (1996a) *Protecting the Public Purse: Ensuring Probity in the NHS (1996 Update)*. Abingdon: Audit Commission Publications.

Audit Commission (1996b) *Protecting the Public Purse: Ensuring Probity in Local Government*. Abingdon: Audit Commission Publications.

Badaracco, J.L. jun. and Webb, A.P. (1995) Business ethics: a view from the trenches. *California Management Review*, 37 (2): 8–28.

Barber, B. (1983) *The Logic and Limits of Trust*. New Brunswick, NJ: Rutgers University Press.

Barnard, C.I. (1938) *The Functions of the Executive*. Cambridge, MA: Harvard University Press.

Benveniste, G. (1987) *Professionalizing the Organization*. San Francisco: Jossey-Bass.

Bernstein, R.J. (1976) *The Restructuring of Social and Political Theory*. Oxford: Blackwell.

Bertilsson, M. (1990) The welfare state, the professions and citizens, in R. Torstendahl and M. Burrage (eds) *The Formulation of Professions, State and Strategy*. London: Sage.

Bok, S. (1995) *Common Values*. Missouri: University of Missouri Press.

Bridges, Sir E. (1950) *Portrait of a Profession*. Cambridge: Cambridge University Press.

Cabinet Office (1993) *Career Management and Succession Planning Study*, (The Oughton Report). London: HMSO.

Cabinet Office (1995) *The Civil Service: Taking Forward Continuity and Change*, Cm. 2748. London: HMSO.

Caiden, G.E., Halley, A.A. and Maltais, D. (1995) Results and lessons from Canada's PS2000. *Public Administration and Development*, 15: 85–102.

Campbell, C. and Halligan, J. (1992) *Political Leadership in an Age of Constraint: Bureaucratic Politics under Hawke and Keating*. St Leonards, New South Wales: Allen & Unwin.

Carter, N. (1989) Performance indicators: 'backseat driving' or 'hands off' control? *Policy and Politics*, 17 (2): 131–8.

Catron, B.L. and Denhardt, K.G. (1994) Ethics education in public administration, in T.L. Cooper (ed.) *Handbook of Administrative Ethics*. New York: Marcel Dekker Inc.

Chapman, R.A. (1995) The first report on standards in public life. *Teaching Public Administration*, XV (2): 1–4.

Chapman, R.A. and Greenaway, J.R. (1980) *The Dynamics of Administrative Reform*. London: Croom Helm.

Colebatch, H.K. (1995) Organizational meanings of program evaluation. *Policy Sciences*, 28: 149–64.

Committee of Public Accounts (1994) Eighth report, *The Proper Conduct of Public Business*. London: HMSO.

Confucius, the *Analects*. Translated with an introduction by B.C. Lau. London: Penguin, 1979.

Conway, D. (1993) The day of the manager. *Community Care*, 19 August: 20–1.

Crowther Hunt, Lord (1980) Mandarins and ministers. *Parliamentary Affairs*, 33: 373–99.

Danley, J., Harrick, E., Schaefer, D. and Sullivan, G. (1996) HR's view of ethics in the work place: are the barbarians at the gate? *Journal of Business Ethics*, 15: 273–85.

Dasgupta, P. (1988) Trust as a commodity, in D. Gambetta (ed.) *Trust: Making and Breaking Co-operative Relations*. Oxford: Blackwell.

Dawson, A.J. (1994) Professional codes of practice and ethical conduct. *Journal of Applied Philosophy*, 11 (2): 145–53.

Denhardt, D.G. (1991) Unearthing the moral foundations of public administration: honor, benevolence and justice, in J.S. Bowman (ed.) *Ethical Frontiers in Public Management*. San Francisco: Jossey-Bass.

Denhardt, K. (1988) *The Ethics of Public Service: Resolving Moral Dilemmas in Public Organisations*. London: Greenwood Press.

Dobel, J.P. (1990) Integrity in the public service. *Public Administration Review*, 50 (3): 354–66.

Dodgson, M. (1993) Organizational learning: a review of some literatures. *Organization Studies*, 14 (3): 375–94.

Doig, A. (1995) Mixed signals? Public sector change and the proper conduct of public business. *Public Administration*, 37 (summer): 191–212.

Douglas, D. (1996) The ethics of managing people. *Business Ethics: A European Review*, 5 (3): 139–42.

Downie, R.S. (1964) *Government Action and Morality*. London: Macmillan.

Downs, A. (1967) *Inside Bureaucracy*. Boston: Little, Brown.

du Gay, P., Salaman, G. and Rees, B. (1996) The conduct of management and the management of conduct: contemporary managerial discourse and the constitution of the 'competent' manager. *Journal of Management Studies*, 33 (3): 263–82.

Dunleavy, P. (1991) *Democracy, Bureaucracy and Public Choice*. Hemel Hempstead: Harvester Wheatsheaf.

Dunleavy, P. and Hood, C. (1994) From old public administration to new public management. *Public Money and Management*, 14 (3): 9–16.

Efficiency Unit (1988) *Improving Management in Government: The Next Steps*. London: HMSO.

Efficiency Unit (1991) Making the Most of Next Steps: *The Management of Ministers' Departments and their Executive Agencies*, the Fraser Report. London: HMSO.

Erlichman, J. (1988) Whistleblowers saved from a US gulag, *Guardian*, 28 July.

Fisher, Sir W. (1928) *Report of the Board of Enquiry Appointed by the Prime Minister to Investigate Statements Affecting Civil Servants*, Cmd. 3037. London: HMSO.

Fox, A. (1974) *Beyond Contract: Work, Power and Trust Relations*. London: Faber & Faber.

Fukuyama, F. (1995) *Trust: The Social Virtues and the Creation of Prosperity*. London: Hamish Hamilton.

Fulton, Lord (1968) *Report of the Committee on the Civil Service*, Cmnd. 3538. London: HMSO.

Gabarro, J.J. (1978) The development of trust, influence and expectations, in A.G. Athos and J.J. Gabarro (eds) *Interpersonal Behaviour: Communication and Understanding in Relationships*. Englewood Cliffs, NJ: Prentice-Hall.

Galbraith, J.K. (1993) *The Culture of Contentment*. Harmondsworth: Penguin.

Gillon, R. (1994) Medical ethics: four principles plus attention to scope. *British Medical Journal*, 309 (16 July): 184–8.

Gilman, S.C. and Lewis, C.W. (1996) Public service ethics: a global dialogue. *Public Administration Review*, 56 (6): 517–24.

Golembiewski, R.T. (1992) Excerpts from *Organization as a Moral Problem*. *Public Administration Review*, 52 (2): 95–8.

Good, D. (1988) Individuals, interpersonal relations and trust, in D. Gambetta (ed.) *Trust: Making and Breaking Co-operative Relations*. Oxford: Blackwell.

Goodsell, C.T. (1994) *The Case for Bureaucracy: A Public Administration Polemic*, 3rd edn. Chatham, NJ: Chatham House.

Gore, A. Jr. (1994) The new job of the federal executive. *Public Administration Review*, 54 (4): 317–21.

Gortner, H. (1991) *Ethics for Public Managers*. New York: Greenwood Press.

Gowler, D. and Legge, K. (1996) The meaning of management and the management of meaning, in S. Linstead, R.G. Small and P. Jeffcutt (eds) *Understanding Management*. London: Sage.

Gyford, J. (1993) *Professionalism, Managerialism and Politics: An Uneasy Co-existence*, Belgrave Papers no. 10. Luton: LGMB.

Hales, C.P. (1986) What do managers do? A critical review of the evidence. *Journal of Management Studies*, 23 (1): 88–115.

Hansard (1994) vol. 264, col 758, 25 October. London: HMSO.

Harrison, S. and Pollitt, C. (1994) *Controlling Health Professionals: The Future of Work and Organization in the NHS*. Buckingham: Open University Press.

Heclo, H. and Wildavsky, A. (1981) *The Private Government of Public Money*, 2nd edn. London: Macmillan.

Hejka-Ekins, A. (1994) Ethics in interservice training, in T.L. Cooper (ed.) *Handbook of Administrative Ethics*. New York: Marcel Dekker.

Hennessy, P. (1990) *Whitehall*. London: Fontana.

Hennessy, P. (1996) *The Hidden Wiring: Unearthing the British Constitution*. London: Indigo.

Hetzner, C. and Schmidt, V.A. (1986) Bringing moral values back in: the role of formal philosophy in affective public administration. *International Journal of Public Administration*, 8 (4): 429–53.

Higher Education Quality Council (1996) *Code of Practice for Overseas Collaborative Provision in Higher Education 1996*, 2nd edn. London: HEQC.

Hodgkinson, C. (1978) *Towards a Philosophy of Administration*. Oxford: Basil Blackwell.

Hood, C. (1996) Beyond 'progressivism': a new 'global paradigm' in public management? *International Journal of Public Administration*, 19 (2): 151–77.

Hopkins, W.E. (1997) *Ethical Dimensions of Diversity*. Newbury Park, CA: Sage.

Hosmer, L.T. (1994) Strategic planning as if ethics mattered. *Strategic Management Journal*, 15: 17–34.

Hummel, R.P. (1987) *The Bureaucratic Experience*, 3rd edn. New York: St Martins Press.

Hutton, W. (1996) *The State We're In*. London: Vintage.

ICAC (Independent Commission Against Corruption) (1991) *The First Two Years: 19 Key Issues*. Sydney: ICAC.

ICAC (Independent Commission Against Corruption) (1997) *Corruption Matters*, 5 (March/April).

Ives, D. (1994) *Submission to the Review of the Public Services Act 1992*. Canberra: Australian Government Publishing Service.

Jabbra, J.G. and Jabbra, N.W. (1983) Public service ethics in the Third World: a comparative perspective, in K. Kernaghan and O.P. Dwivedi (eds) *Ethics in the Public Service: Comparative Perspectives*. Brussels: International Institute of Administrative Sciences.

Jackson, M.W. (1993) How can ethics be taught? in R.A. Chapman (ed.) *Ethics in Public Service*. Edinburgh: Edinburgh University Press.

Jennings, B. (1991) The regulation of virtue: cross-currents in professional ethics. *Journal of Business Ethics*, 10: 561–8.

Johnson, N. (1994) Institutions and human relations: a search for stability in a changing world. *American Behavioral Scientist*, 38 (1): 26–42.

Joint Committee of Public Accounts (1992) *Managing People in the Australian Public Service, Dilemmas of Devolution and Diversity*. Canberra: Australian Government Publishing Service.

Jones, W.T. (1984) Public roles, private roles and differential moral assessments of role performance. *Ethics*, 94: 603–20.

Jos, P.H. and Hines, S.M. (1993) Care, justice and public administration. *Administration and Society*, 25 (3): 373–92.

Kanter, R.M. and Summers, D.V. (1987) Doing well while doing good: dilemmas of performance measurement in nonprofit organizations and the need for a multiple-constituency approach, in W.W. Powell (ed.) *The Nonprofit Sector: A Research Handbook*. New Haven, CT: Yale University Press.

Kernaghan, K. (1975) *Ethical Conduct: Guidelines for Government Employees*. Toronto: Institute of Public Administration.

Kernaghan, K. (1993a) Promoting public service ethics: the codification option, in R.A. Chapman (ed.) *Ethics in Public Service*. Edinburgh: Edinburgh University Press.

Kernaghan, K. (1993b) Partnership and public administration: conceptual and practical considerations. *Canadian Public Administration*, 36 (1): 57–76.

Keynes, J.M. (1936) *The General Theory of Employment, Interest and Money*. London: Macmillan.

Kohlberg, L. (1976) Moral stages and moralization: the cognitive development approach, in T. Lickona (ed.) *Moral Development and Behaviour: Theory, Research and Social Issues*. New York: Holt, Rinehart and Winston.

Lebacqz, K. (1985) *Professional Ethics*. Nashville, TN: Abingdon Press.

Leigh, D. and Vulliamy, E. (1997) *Sleaze: The Corruption of Parliament*. London: Fourth Estate.

Lewis, C.W. (1991) *The Ethics Challenge in Public Service: A Problem-Solving Guide*. San Francisco: Jossey-Bass.

Lilla, M. (1981) Ethos, ethics and the public service. *Public Interest*, spring: 3–17.

Local Government Management Board (undated) *Code of Conduct for Local Government Employees*. Luton: LGMB.

Local Government Management Board (1993) *Fitness for Purpose*. Luton: LGMB.

Locke, J. (1960) *Two Treatises 'Of Government'*, with an introduction by P. Laslett. Cambridge: Cambridge University Press.

Longenecker, C. and Ludwig, D. (1990) Ethical dilemmas in performance appraisal revisited. *Journal of Business Ethics*, 9: 961–9.

Luhmann, N. (1979) *Trust and Power*. Chichester: John Wiley & Sons.

MacIntyre, A. (1981) *After Virtue: A Study in Moral Theory*. London: Duckworth.

McKevitt, D. and Lawton, A. (1996) The manager, the citizen, the politician and performance measures. *Public Money and Management*, 16 (3): 49–54.

Mackintosh, M. (1995) *Putting words into people's mouths? Economic culture and its implications for local governance*, open discussion paper in economics, no. 9. Milton Keynes: Faculty of Social Sciences, The Open University.

MacLagan, P. (1995) Ethical thinking in organizations: implications for management education. *Management Learning*, 26 (2): 159–77.

Madron, R. (1995) Performance improvement in public services. *Political Quarterly*, 66 (3): 181–94.

Maheshwari, S.R. (1983) Public service ethics in India, in K. Kernaghan and O. Dwivedi (eds) *Ethics in the Public Service: Comparative Perspectives*. Brussels: International Institute of Administrative Sciences.

Management Advisory Board (1993) *Building a Better Public Service*. Canberra: Australian Government Publishing Service.

Management Advisory Board (1996) *Ethical Standards and Values in the Australian Public Service*. Canberra: Australian Government Publishing Service.

Mayston, D.J. (1985) Non-profit performance indicators in the public sector. *Financial Accountability and Management*, 11 (1): 51–74.

Metcalfe, L. and Richards, S. (1990) *Improving Public Management*, 2nd edn. London: Sage.

Mintzberg, H. (1983) *Power in and around Organizations*. Englewood Cliffs, NJ: Prentice-Hall.

Mintzberg, H. (1996) Managing government, governing management. *Harvard Business Review*, May/June: 75–83.

MORI (1996) *First Division Association (Crown Prosecution Service Section) Survey*. Research study conducted for the Association of First Division Civil Servants, July–September.

Murray, M. (1975) Comparing public and private management: an exploratory essay. *Public Administration Review*, 35 (4): 364–71.

Nash, L. (1981) Ethics without the sermon. *Harvard Business Review*, November/December: 79–90.

National Institute for Social Work (1997) *Work-based Learning*, Bulletin No. 1. London: NISW.

Nolan Committee (1995) *Standards in Public Life*, Volume 1. First report of the committee on standards in public life. London: HMSO.

Nolan Committee (1997) *Standards of Conduct in Local Government in England, Scotland and Wales*, Cm 3702–I. Third report on standards in public life. London: The Stationery Office.

Norris, C. and Norris, N. (1993) Defining good policing: the instrumental and moral approaches to good practice and competence. *Policing and Society*, 3 (3): 205–21.

Oakeshott, M. (1962) *Rationalism in Politics and Other Essays*. London: Methuen.

OECD (1994) *Performance Management in Government: Performance Measurement and Results-oriented Management*, Public Management Occasional Papers No. 3. Paris: OECD.

OECD (1995) *Governance in Transition: Public Management Reforms in OECD Countries*. Paris: OECD.

OECD (1996) *Ethics in the Public Service: Current Issues and Practice*, public management occasional papers no. 14. Paris: OECD.

Open University (1993) 'The Design and Control of Public Markets', Managing Public Services (B887), Unit 5. Milton Keynes: OUEE.

Osborne, D. and Gaebler, T. (1992) *Reinventing Government: How the Entrepreneurial Spirit is Transforming the Public Sector*. Reading, MA: Addison-Wesley.

Peters, B. (1991) Morale in the public service: a comparative inquiry. *International Review of Administrative Sciences*, 57: 421–40.

Plowden, W. (1985) What prospects for the Civil Service? *Public Administration*, 63 (4): 393–414.

Plowden, W. (1994) *Ministers and Mandarins*. London: Institute for Public Policy Research.

Pollitt, C. (1987) The politics of performance assessment: lessons for higher education. *Studies in Higher Education*, 12 (1): 87–98.

Pollitt, C. (1993) *Managerialism and the Public Services: Cuts or Cultural Change in the 1990s?*, 2nd edn. Oxford: Blackwell.

Popper, K. (ed.) (1966) *The Open Society and its Enemies*, vols 1 and 2. London: Routledge and Kegan Paul.

Pops, G.M. (1994) A teleological approach to administrative ethics, in T.L. Cooper (ed.) *Handbook of Administrative Ethics*. New York: Marcel Dekker Inc.

Pratchett, L. and Wingfield, M. (1994) *The Public Service Ethos in Local Government: A Research Report*. London: CLD Ltd with ICSA.

Public Concern at Work (1995) *Creating the Right Environment: A Checklist for Employees*. London: Public Concern at Work.

Pugh, D.L. (1991) The origins of ethical frameworks in public administration, in J.S. Bowman (ed.) *Ethical Frontiers in Public Management: Seeking New Strategies for Resolving Ethical Dilemmas*. San Francisco, CA: Jossey-Bass.

Pusey, M. (1991) *Economic Rationalism in Canberra: A Nation Building State Changes its Mind*. Cambridge: Cambridge University Press.

Quinlan, Sir M. (1993) Ethics in the public service. *Governance: An International Journal of Policy and Administration*, 6 (4): 538–44.

Quinlan, Sir M. (1995) Oral evidence given to the Nolan Committee, in Nolan Committee *Standards in Public Life*, vol. 2 *Transcripts of Oral Evidence*, p. 239. London: HMSO.

Rainey, H.G., Backoff, R.W. and Levine, C.H. (1976) Comparing public and private organizations. *Public Administration Review*, 36 (2): 233–44.

Ranson, S. and Stewart, J. (1994) *Management for the Public Domain: Enabling the Learning Society*. Basingstoke: Macmillan.

Rawls, J. (1972) *A Theory of Justice*. Oxford: Oxford University Press.

Redcliffe-Mand, Lord (1979) *Conduct in Local Government*, Cmnd 5636. London: HMSO.

Rees, S. (1995) Greed and bullying, in S. Rees and G. Rodley (eds) *The Human Costs of Managerialism*. Leichhardt, Australia: Pluto Press.

Reiser, S.J. (1994) The ethical life of health care organizations. *Hastings Center Report*, 24 (6): 28–35.

Richards, N. (1996) A plea for applied ethics, in R. Thomas (ed.) *Teaching Ethics*, vol. 1 *Government Ethics*. London: HMSO and Ethics International Press Ltd, Cambridge.

Ridley, F.F. (1983) The British Civil Service and politics: principles in question and traditions in flux. *Parliamentary Affairs*, 56: 28–48.

Ridley, F.F. (1987) What are the duties and responsibilities of civil servants? *Public Administration*, 65 (1): 79–87.

Roberston, D.C. and Schlegelmilch, B.B. (1993) Corporate institutionalization of ethics in the United States and Great Britain. *Journal of Business Ethics*, 12: 301–12.

Rohr, J. (1978) *Ethics for Bureaucrats*. New York: Marcel Dekker Inc.

Salmon, Lord (1976) *Royal Commission on Standards of Conduct in Public Affairs*, Cmnd 6524. London: HMSO.

Schein, E. (1987) *Organizational Culture and Leadership*. San Francisco: Jossey-Bass.

Schlegelmilch, B.B. and Houston, J.E. (1990) Corporate codes of ethics. *Management Decision*, 28 (7): 38–43.

Schön, D.A. (1983) *The Reflective Practitioner: How Professionals Think in Action*. New York: Basic Books.

Schroder, H.M. (1989) *Managerial Competences: The Key to Excellence*. Dubuque: Kendall Hunt.

Self, P. (1977) *Administrative Theories and Politics: An Enquiry into the Structure and Processes of Modern Government*. London: Allen & Unwin.

Senge, P. (1990) *The Fifth Discipline*. New York: Random Books.

Sharpe, L.J. (1985) Central co-ordination and the policy network. *Political Studies*, 33: 361–81.

Sinclair, A. (1993) Approaches to organisational culture and ethics. *Journal of Business Ethics*, 12: 63–73.

Sisson, C.H. (1959) *The Spirit of British Administration*. London: Faber & Faber.

Soutar, G.N., McNeil, M. and Molster, C. (1995) A management perspective on business ethics. *Journal of Business Ethics*, 14: 603–11.

Steinberg, S.S. and Austen, D.T. (1990) *Government Ethics and Managers: A Guide to Solving Ethical Dilemmas in the Public Sector*. Westport, CT: Quorum Books.

Sternberg, E. (1994) *Just Business: Business Ethics in Action*. London: Warner Books.

Stewart, J.D. (1989) In search of curriculum for management for the public sector. *Management Education and Development*, 20 (3): 168–75.

Stewart, J.D. and Ranson, S. (1988) Management in the public domain. *Public Money and Management*, spring/summer: 13–19.

Stoker, G. (1993) Professions, accountability and the new local governance, in Belgrave Papers no. 10 *The Future of Professionalism in Local Government*. Luton: LGMB.

Suzuki, P.T. (1995) Public sector ethics in comparative perspective, in *The Annals of the American Academy of Political and Social Science*, vol. 537 (special edition): H.W. Reynolds (ed.) *Ethics in American Public Service*, pp. 173–83.

Thompson, D.F. (1980) Moral responsibility of public officials: the problem of many hands. *The American Political Science Review*, 74: 905–16.

Thucydides, *History of the Peloponnesian War*. Harmondsworth: Penguin, 1954.

Travers, T. (1993) Professionalism and local government reform: not so much villains as saviours, in Belgrave Papers no. 10 *The Future of Professionalism in Local Government*. Luton: LGMB.

Treasury and Civil Service Committee (1986) Seventh report, *Civil Servants and Ministers: Duties and Responsibilities*. London: HMSO.

Treasury and Civil Service Committee (1989) *Developments in the Next Steps Programme*. London: HMSO.

Treasury and Civil Service Committee (1994a) Fifth report, *The Role of the Civil Service*, vol. 1. London: HMSO.

Treasury and Civil Service Committee (1994b) *The Role of the Civil Service*, vol. 1 and minutes of evidence. London: HMSO.

Uhr, J. (1991) The ethics debate: five framework propositions. *Australian Journal of Public Administration*, 50 (3): 285–91.

Van Maanen, J. and Barley, S.R. (1984) Occupational communities: culture and control in organizations. *Research in Organizational Behaviour*, 6: 287–365.

Vickers, Sir G. (1965) *The Art of Judgement: A Study of Policy Making*. London: Chapman & Hall.

Wanna, J., O'Faircheallaigh, C. and Weller, P. (1992) *Public Sector Management in Australia*. Melbourne: Macmillan.

Wass, Sir D. (1983) The public service in modern society. *Public Administration*, 61: 7–20.

Watson, T.J. (1996) How do managers think? Identity, morality and pragmatism in managerial theory and practice. *Management and Learning*, 27 (3): 323–41.

Watt, D.C. (1988) The public interest in question: industry as clients and constituents of government departments. *Political Quarterly*, 59 (1): 56–62.

Weber, M. (1968) *Economy and Society*. New York: Bedminster Press.

Weir, S. and Hall, W. (1994) *EGO Trip: Extra-governmental Organisations in the United Kingdom and their Accountability*. London: Charter 88 Trust.

Williamson, O. (1975) *Markets and Hierarchies: Analysis and Anti-trust Implications*. New York: Free Press.

Winstanley, D. and Stuart-Smith, K. (1996) Policing performance: the ethics of performance management. *Personnel Review*, 25 (6): 66–83.

Wittgenstein, L. (1953) *Philosophical Investigations*. Blackwell: Oxford.

Wrigley, L. and McKevitt, D. (1994) Professional ethics, government agenda and differential information, in A. Lawton and D. McKevitt (eds) *Public Sector Management: Theory, Critique and Practice*. London: Sage.

Young, H. (1990) *One of Us*. London: Pan.

Young, H. and Sloman, A. (1984) *But Chancellor: An Inquiry into the Treasury*. London: BBC Books.

Zifcak, S. (1994) *New Managerialism: Administrative Reform in Whitehall and Canberra*. Buckingham: Open University Press.

Index

FINANCIAL MANAGEMENT FOR THE PUBLIC SERVICES

John Wilson (ed.)

Written for new and existing managers, undergraduate and postgraduate students of the public services, this essential textbook explores the meaning and significance of financial management for the public services. It combines both theoretical arguments and practical applications, and:

- examines the economics of public services
- considers the extent to which the management of public services has actually changed in practice
- explains the meaning and applicability of financial management tools including those relating to budgets and capital investment
- presents original work on the issue of audit expectations
- presents case studies on the problems which can arise when traditional concerns on probity and stewardship are neglected
- considers the benefits and problems of measuring performance in the public services
- includes specific chapters on financial management in health services and local government.

Contents
Preface – Acknowledgements – Abbreviations – Part one: Public service environment – Economics of public service provision – The new management of public services – Part two: Understanding finance – Budgeting and budgetary control – Costing and pricing in the public sector – Capital investment appraisal – Part three: Applied accountability – Audit quality – The mismanagement of financial resources – Performance measurement – Part four: Key sectors – Local government financial management – National health service financial management – Part five: Towards the future – Financial management: an overview – Index.

304pp   0 335 19845 7 (Paperback)   0 335 19846 5 (Hardback)